Heather Boersma

DREAM
Big

30 Days to a Life
Beyond All You
Could Ask or
Imagine

DREAM BIG
Copyright © 2012 by Heather Boersma

Scriptures taken from the Holy Bible, New International Version®, NIV®. Copyright © 1973, 1978, 1984, 2011 by Biblica, Inc.™ Used by permission of Zondervan. All rights reserved worldwide. The "NIV" and "New International Version" are trademarks registered in the United States Patent and Trademark Office by Biblica, Inc.™

Printed in Canada

Word Alive Press
131 Cordite Road, Winnipeg, MB R3W 1S1
www.wordalivepress.ca

Library and Archives Canada Cataloguing in Publication

Boersma, Heather, 1983-
     Dream big : 30 days to life beyond all you could ask
or imagine / Heather Boersma.

ISBN 978-1-77069-453-8

     1. Youth--Religious life--Juvenile literature. 2. Young
adults--Religious life--Juvenile literature. 3. Youth-Vocational
guidance--Juvenile literature. 4. Young adults--Vocational
guidance--Juvenile literature. 5. Self-actualization (Psychology)--
Religious aspects--Christianity--Juvenile literature. I. Title.

BV4531.3.B63 2012   j248.8'3   C2011-908443-0

For Alex
—my best friend, husband and fellow big dreamer.
I love living this adventure with you.

Table of Contents

I was just one in a crowd of thousands. All around me eyes were glued to the front where the speaker moved across the stage with ease and authority. As she spoke, something in me quickened—a spark was lit. Suddenly ideas, inspiration, and vision for the future flooded my thoughts. In that moment I knew what God wanted me to do with my life! My big dream was born.

Maybe you picked this book up because you have that same feeling of excitement about the big dream God's given you. Or maybe you're still trying to figure out what your big dream is. Either way, I'm excited you are taking a step towards pursuing God's plan for your life because there is nothing like seeing your big dreams come true.

I remember the very first time I had a taste of *living* my big dream. It was a few years after the day I sat in the audience and realized my call in life. Now I was the one standing up in front of six hundred teenagers getting ready to speak. My heart raced with nervous anticipation, excitement and adrenaline. For years I'd been waiting for a chance like this, and now my dream was becoming a reality.

That's why I've written this book! I want you to experience that same joy and fulfillment, and to know God's dream for you is beyond all you could ask or imagine. He doesn't want you to settle for anything less than the abundant life He planned for you before the creation of the world. But how do we figure out what our big dream is, and how do we live it out? This book is designed to help you both discover God's big dream for you and take practical steps to make that dream come true.

How to Use this Book

This book is organized into three main parts. The first part, "God's Dream for the World", outlines some of God's basic desires for His people, both in the Old and New Testament. The second part, called "God's Dream for You", helps you personalize the overarching themes outlined in part one and begin to discover what your big dream is. The third part, "Unlocking Your Dream", describes how an intimate relationship with Jesus is the key to seeing your dreams come to life.

My hope is that this book will take you deeper in your relationship with Christ, to a place where you are able to hear His voice speaking directly to you. I pray you will understand more of who God is and the incredible love He has for you. However, in order for this to happen, I encourage you to make a serious commitment to this 30 day journey. Consider committing to the following for the next 30 days:

- Commit to reading the passages suggested at the beginning of each day, behind the heading "Dream Manual". I've called it this because God's word really is the best place to find practical instructions to make our dreams a reality.
- Commit to answering the questions at the end of each lesson in the "Dream Journal". You can do this right in the book, or get yourself a fresh, new journal to write your reflections in.
- Commit to spending time in prayer at the end of each lesson, guided by the questions outlined in the "Meet with the Dream-Giver" section. I believe God wants to speak to you each and every day, but it's hard to hear from Him if we don't set aside time to listen.
- Commit to applying the things God is teaching you through this study. Obedience is key.

May God bless and keep you as you seek His will for your life for the next 30 days. May He give you the strength and discipline needed to complete this journey with Him.

If at any point in this journey you have questions or comments, or just need someone to listen, feel free to contact me through my facebook page "Heather Boersma - Christian Speaker" or on Twitter @ HeatherBoersma. You can also send an email by going to the "Contact" page on my website, www.heatherboersma.com. To find additional resources about how to pursue God's big dreams for your life, check out my blog at www.heatherboersma.com/blog. I would love to hear from you at any time!

In Him,
Heather

PART ONE

GOD'S DREAM
FOR THE
World

.

God—The Original Big Dreamer

Day 1

"Let all the earth fear the Lord; let all the people of the world revere him. For he spoke, and it came to be; he commanded, and it stood firm. The Lord foils the plans of the nations; he thwarts the purposes of the peoples. But the plans of the Lord stand firm forever, the purposes of his heart through all generations." (Psalm 33:8–11)

Dream Manual: Read Genesis 1 and Psalm 33.

Imagine the day God decided to begin creating. Imagine what went through His mind as He planned out the universe—the galaxies, planets, sun, moon, stars, and earth. Imagine how His thoughts raced as He visualized bright scales on the sides of tropical fish, the spray of colour bursting from the centre of hibiscus flowers, the cascading canopy of willow tree branches. Just look at the detail of your unique fingerprint— there is only one like it—and it's plain to see that God is the original big dreamer. He was the first to dream and the first to see His dreams come true. Psalm 33:6 says, *"By the word of the Lord the heavens were made, their starry host by the breath of his mouth."* Our God lives and breathes big dreams. In fact even *you* were a part of His big dream! When God was creating the world, He ended each day by saying *"It is good"* (Genesis

1

1:10). But did you know that when He made man and woman (us!) He said something different? When God made humans, He said, *"It is very good."* I imagine He smiled as he planned your goofy grin, laughed as he charted the tune of your chuckle, and sighed with satisfaction when you took your first breath. God had big dreams *of you* and *for you* right from the very beginning!

Genesis 1:26–27 confirms that you are indeed created by God but also in the image of God: *"Then God said, 'Let us make man in our image, in our likeness'. . . so God created mankind in his own image, in the image of God he created them; male and female he created them."* What does it mean to be made in the image of God? Well, think of it this way. One day your parents got together and decided to create you. (Gross, I know! Don't think about it for too long!) Because you contain DNA from both of your parents, it can be said that you were made *in their image.* You may have the same eyes as your dad or the same hips as your mom. People often tell me that I look just like my dad and I think, "Great, I look like a 55-year-old man. Excellent! Thanks a bunch." But for real, as children we carry some of the likeness or image of the ones who made us. This same principle applies to God. We are His children! We have some of His "spiritual DNA" built into who we are. Pretty amazing isn't it? And one aspect of God's image or "spiritual DNA" that you carry is the ability to dream. It is natural to dream, plan, and think about the future—to long for a life that is extraordinary. As we spend more time with God and become more like Him, our dreams will likely grow bigger and may seem more impossible to attain.

Look at Joseph, for example. At 17 years old his dreams were so big they almost got him killed by his own brothers! I imagine his brothers thought he was downright crazy (and obnoxious) when he announced that he dreamed that one day the whole family, including his mom and dad, would bow down to him. Why don't you grab your Bible right now and read about Joseph and his wild dreams in Genesis 37:1–11?

It's amazing to think that dreams like the ones Joseph had are actually from God. Telling his brothers about them probably wasn't the wisest thing to do, but it doesn't change the fact that they were *God's dreams* for Joseph. In the end those dreams came true, saving the lives of not only Joseph's family but of an entire nation! A dream that big can only come from God.

Although this devotional isn't about the dreams we have at night, like Joseph's dreams, it is about creating goals with God. One definition of the word *dream* is *"a strongly desired goal or purpose, something that fully satisfies a wish."* That is what this book is all about—equipping you to define and accomplish the purpose God has for your life!

One dream from God can change the course of your entire life. In fact, one dream from God can change the course of history! Isn't that what Jesus' life, death, and resurrection represent—God's biggest dream come true? But how can we know what God's dream for our life is? A great way to begin to define God's dream for you is to look at what His dreams are for all of creation.

Over the next few days we'll examine God's heart and character to identify some of the over-arching desires He has for the world He created, looking first at the Old Testament and then at the New Testament. If you want to live a life full of adventure, purpose, and abundance, then getting to know God and His dreams is an excellent first step. *"But the plans of the Lord stand firm forever, the purposes of his heart through all generations"* (Psalm 33:11). According to this verse, God's original dream for creation is the same today as it was the day He first created, and the purposes of his heart *will* be accomplished. The question is, are you ready to be a part of His big dream?

Dream Journal

1. Describe one aspect of creation that makes you think of God as a big dreamer?

2. What does it mean to you to know that you were a part of God's original big dream?

3. How was God's dream for Joseph beneficial not only to Joseph but to his entire family and the nation of Egypt?

4. What does that teach you about God's dreams?

5. In what ways are you a big dreamer like God?

Meet the Dream-Giver

1. Imagine yourself in the Garden of Eden with God. Where would He be?

2. What expression would be on His face? Why?

3. Ask God to tell you about what was going through His mind as He made creation. What would He say?

4. Now ask him what He was thinking when He made you. What would He say?

4

Day 2

"Love the Lord your God with all your heart and with all your soul and with all your strength." (Deuteronomy 6:5)

Dream Manual: Read Genesis 12:1–9 and Genesis 15.

The first section of this book is called "God's Dream for the World." For the first 11 days of this 30-day journey, we'll spend some time doing an overview of the Old and New Testaments, looking for some of God's specific dreams for humanity. The Old Testament will help us to define what God's original design was and how He responded when things didn't go according to His plan. The New Testament will outline God's unique dream for the church, communicated specifically through Jesus while He walked the earth. By looking at God's dreams in the Old and New Testaments, we'll be better prepared to hear from Him about His specific dreams for *our* lives in part 2 of this book.

Do you ever feel like God is hiding His will from you? I've often heard people say, "What's God's will for my life? What does He want me to do after high school? Where does He want me to live? Why can't He just tell me if I should break up with my boyfriend or girlfriend?" My response to these questions is this: *God does not want to hide His will from you.* He has a plan to prosper you and not to harm you, to give you hope and a future (Jeremiah 29:11). But sometimes we have to get to know Him through His word to understand more clearly what His plan is. Everything God wanted us to know about Him was written in His word. Have you ever thought about that before? The Bible is inspired by God, and it is our best tool to help us know Him more and understand Him more deeply. He could have chosen to make the Bible as long or as short as He wanted. He could've included illustrations of Himself if He saw fit. He could have made the Bible one book or one thousand books. But He didn't. Exactly what He wanted us to know He revealed through His word, the Bible. So if we want to know what His will is, we need to first search His word for clues.

First and foremost, God's dream is to be in perfect relationship with us. When God first created humans, Genesis 3:8 says He *"was walking in the garden in the cool of the day."* He was physically walking *with* Adam and Eve. His ideal plan and design was to be with us in every way possible, including physically. Imagine how different your relationship with Him would be had things gone according to this plan! Many of the challenges we face in our friendship with God are directly related to the fact that we can't experience Him physically.

Even though things didn't turn out exactly as God first dreamed, His desire remains the same. He wants to know you. He wants to be your best friend. He wants to have an intimate relationship with you. We can see this desire all throughout the Old Testament in His relationship with the Israelites, His chosen people. It's particularly clear in the words He spoke when He first called Abraham. Have a look: *"I will make you into a great nation and I will bless you; I will make your name great and you will be a blessing. I will bless those who bless you, and whoever curses you I will curse; and all people on earth will be blessed through you* (Genesis 12:2–3).*"* This passage powerfully demonstrates God's desire for relationship with both the individual (Abraham) and all of humanity ("all people on earth"). He longs to bless us, use us to bless others, and protect us from anyone who may be against us!

After the fall of Adam and Eve in the garden of Eden, God could've given up on humanity. In fact He almost did when He brought the great flood. But His heart was and ever is moved by compassion for us, so He spared Noah and his family. Psalm 103:8 says, *"The Lord is compassionate and gracious, slow to anger, abounding in love."* If ever someone had a reason to give up on someone, God had reason to give up on us. But He didn't. Instead He graciously gave us another chance.

How about you? Have you given up on Him? Have you allowed the things of the world to distract you or even drag you away from His loving embrace? Have you settled for less than His best? My hope is that during this 30-day journey you would come to know God in a deeper, more intimate way than ever before. I hope you can see His heart for you in a new light. And I pray you can dream with Him for a life beyond all you could ask or imagine.

Dream Journal
1. Why do you think God chose to spare humanity even after Adam and Eve's fall in the garden of Eden?

2. What is the significance of God's words to Abraham in Genesis 12:3: *"I will bless those who bless you and whoever curses you I will curse"*?

3. How is your relationship with God right now? How would you like to grow and improve it over the next 28 days?

Meet the Dream-Giver
1. Ask God to show you one way He'd like to be closer to you today.

2. Especially if you're struggling to hear His voice, ask Him if there is anything standing in the way of you becoming closer to Him.

3. If He shows you something that is blocking your relationship with Him, ask Him how He wants to get rid of that obstacle.

Day 3

"This day I call the heavens and the earth as witnesses against you that I have set before you life and death, blessings and curses. Now choose life, so that you and your children may live." (Deuteronomy 30:19)

Dream Manual: Read Exodus 20:1–21 or Deuteronomy 5:1–32.
One of God's dreams for us, found in the Old Testament, is for us to live the very best lives possible. He is truly a loving Father who wants His children to be fulfilled, safe, and content. But God is also all-knowing and sees our faults, weaknesses, and selfish tendencies, which sometimes keep us from the best life. Because He loves us and wants to prevent us from going off track, He gives us rules to help us.

Many of us really don't like the word "rules." Especially in our teenage and young adult years, as we begin to assert our independence, the idea of "following the rules" leaves a foul taste in our mouths. Why is this? Perhaps it's because we've experienced people like our parents or teachers using rules to try and control us.

But God's reason for giving us guidelines is absolutely not because He wants to control us. If that was His desire, why would He have given us free will in the first place? One of the most powerful abilities God gave us is the power to choose. But He does offer us help as we navigate the multitude of choices we face in this life.

I like to think of it this way. I spent a couple of summers working as a wakeboard coach at a few bible camps in Canada. My role as a coach was to help the campers I was training achieve the most success possible in the sport of wake boarding. I wanted them to get up, have fun, and most important, not get hurt. Because those were my goals (very similar to God's goals for us in this life), I gave each camper rules to help them. If I had just strapped a board on them, dumped 'em in the water and said "Good luck," a few may have been successful. But most would've failed, and some may have been injured. However, when I laid out the basic rules, such as "Knees bent, arms straight, and let the boat pull you up," many of them got up on their first try and had fun! The rules weren't there to control them, but to set them up for success and the best experience possible.

God is the best coach. His dream for all of us, His children, is to experience this life to the fullest. John 10:10 says, *"I have come that they* (that's you!) *may have life, and have it to the full."* This is why God gave His people, the Israelites, the Ten Commandments, as we can read in Exodus 20. And if you look closely at the guidelines God set out, it's clear His desire is not to control us but to help us have thriving relationships, both with Himself and others.

Let's look at Exodus 20:1–12 again. The first four commandments are all focused on helping us have a closer, deeper relationship with God. Each one directs us to an action that increases our respect for God. For example, verse 7 says, *"You shall not misuse the name of the Lord your God."* Maybe you think saying "Oh, my God" is no big deal, but does it show respect to God? And if we lose respect for the name of God, what will happen to our relationship with Him? James 3:10–11 says, *"Out of the same mouth come praise and cursing. My brothers and sisters, this should not be. Can both fresh water and salt water flow from the same spring?"* It's really quite hypocritical of us to praise God's name on Sunday and use it in vain Monday morning. Not only is doing so a bad witness, but it shows a lack of respect for God and keeps us from a deeper level of intimacy with Him. Most often the people we have the closest relationships with are those *we respect the most.* God wants that kind of relationship with you.

Just as the first four commandments are about closeness with God, the last six are about closeness with others. For example, verse 12 says, *"Honor your Father and Mother, so that you may live long in the land the Lord your God is giving you."* God sees the bigger picture. He knows that if we dishonor our parents in a moment of rage or frustration, we may regret our decision later. Many of us don't have the blessing of a close relationship with our parents, but I don't know one person who doesn't hope for that. God knows that this relationship is important and that when it's strong, we are blessed because of it. So He commands us to honor our parents, even when it's hard. By honoring them, we honor Him as well.

One of God's primary dreams for humanity is for each of us to enjoy the blessing of right relationships with Him and with others. Because of this desire, He gives us the Ten Commandments, and if we're obedient to them, they will set us up for the best, most fulfilling life possible.

Dream Journal

1. Which commandment do you struggle the most to follow? Why?

2. Why is mutual respect important in our relationship with God and others? What happens when we don't have that respect?

3. What does Exodus 20:19 tell us about why God wants us to respect/ fear Him?

Meet the Dream-Giver

1. Ask God to show you what your attitude toward "following the rules" is?

2. Ask him, "Which one of the 10 commandments could I work on this week, and how will it bring me closer to your big dreams for my life?"

Day 4

"If it is possible, as far as it depends on you, live at peace with everyone." (Romans 12:18)

Dream Manual: Read Leviticus 25:8–56.

Second only to God's dream of a close relationship with you is His desire for us to have right relationships with one another, which we touched on briefly yesterday. He wants all of us, His children, to just get along. We can see this dream reflected in the 10 Commandments and all over the Old Testament. A huge part of staying in right relationships with each other is practicing forgiveness, even when we feel the other person doesn't deserve it.

For some of you the topic of forgiveness is more complicated than for others. Some of you have been through terrible injustices in your lives, and the idea of forgiving those who've hurt you seems nearly impossible. This is how Jacqui from British Columbia, Canada must have felt when her older brother brutally beat her and her father and then killed their mother. However, even after this horrible and traumatic injustice, Jacqui chose to forgive her brother and now speaks about forgiveness to different groups across Canada. And the most astonishing

13

thing is that when she speaks, she often brings her brother along! Talk about radical forgiveness!

God dreamed that His chosen people, the Israelites, would be a people of radical forgiveness and pursue right relationships with each other. In order to help them become those people, He created an event (well, a whole year actually) called "The Year of Jubilee," described in the passage you read today. It's a long and slightly confusing passage, but the principle it outlines is revolutionary and important for us if we want to understand God's dreams for humanity more fully.

Essentially "The Year of Jubilee" was a time when the slate was wiped clean. All past debts were forgiven, slaves were set free, and property was returned to its original owner. Though this event only happened every 50 years, it was a really great year for some and a really challenging one for others. For those who were in debt, enslaved, and poor, this year was the biggest second chance ever—like someone hitting the reset button on life just in time. Alternatively, for those who were prospering, those with households full of servants, and those waiting to receive payment from their debtors, this was a bad year. Not only did they have to set their slaves free, they could forget about ever getting their money back from those who owed them.

How would you handle a relational "Year of Jubilee" right about now? A year in which you let go of all past hurts, forgave all who had wronged you, and hit the reset button on all of your relationships? Would you be relieved to know *your* past mistakes would be forgiven, or would you feel cheated because you wouldn't get the justice you deserve? This is exactly what God dreams of for us—a Year of Jubilee for our relationships. A fresh start. Not only does He dream of this, but He commands it! Why is this principle so important to God? Here are a couple of verses in Leviticus 25 to help explain:

> vs. 17 *"Do not take advantage of each other, but fear your God. I am the Lord your God."*
> vs. 38 *"I am the Lord your God, who brought you out of Egypt to give you the land of Canaan and to be your God."*
> vs. 42–43 *"Because the Israelites are my servants, whom I brought*

out of Egypt, they must not be sold as slaves. Do not rule over them ruthlessly, but fear your God."

vs. 54–55 *"Even if someone is not redeemed in any of these ways, they and their children are to be released in the Year of Jubilee, for the Israelites belong to me as servants. They are my servants, whom I brought out of Egypt. I am the Lord your God."*

Do you understand God's way a little better now? God is reminding the Israelites that they were all slaves until He set them free. We too were all slaves to sin until Jesus came and set us free by His radical forgiveness. We forgive because He first forgave us. We let go of the past because He let go of ours. We set those free who've wronged us because God set us free when we wronged Him! Wow. How can we argue with that? We don't have a leg to stand on, and I'm glad. This kind of forgiveness doesn't just bring freedom to those we forgive: it sets us free too! Maybe today is the day to start your own personal Year of Jubilee.

Dream Journal

1. Who are some people who you feel "owe" you and haven't paid up?

2. How can you apply the Year of Jubilee to your life today and to these relationships?

3. Why is it difficult to forgive those who've hurt us or shown us injustice?

Meet the Dream-Giver

1. Ask God to bring to mind one or two people with whom you need to "settle accounts."

2. Ask Jesus why you should forgive and let go of those hurts. What reason does He give you?

UNITY WITH CREATION

Day 5

"Let all creation rejoice before the Lord, for he comes, he comes to judge the earth. He will judge the world in righteousness and the peoples in his faithfulness." (Psalm 96:13)

Dream Manual: Read Psalm 148.

God loves His creation—not just humans but every created thing. 1 Timothy 4:4 says *"For everything God created is good, and nothing is to be rejected if it is received with thanksgiving."* Everything God created is good, and this verse demonstrates God's desire for us to have respect and gratitude for all He created.

We live in a time when it is very trendy to be "green" and "organic" and "eco-friendly." But this idea is not new or unique to our generation. It reflects a piece of God's heart for the earth. It's a desire He's had since the beginning of time. But His perspective is a little different from the world's. God doesn't want us to be "green" because the earth needs to last forever. It's not about global warming for Him. He wants to use all of creation to teach us, bless us, and sustain us until He comes again and brings *"a new heaven and a new earth"* (2 Peter 3:13). The earth is not ours, but it's been put in our care and stewardship for a time and a reason.

CREATION TEACHES US TO WORSHIP

In Psalm 148, King David reflects on how all the elements of creation praise God simply by being what God created them to be: the sun, moon, stars; the ocean, mountains, and animals. All of them set an example for us of how to worship God. We worship not by striving to be something, but simply by being.

God often speaks to me through creation. Some of my most memorable times with the Lord have been at my family cabin, staring out over the glassy lake or up at the starry night sky. When I see the beauty of creation, praise and admiration for God is a natural reaction. And when I'm not physically surrounded by nature, God often gives me pictures of His love in the form of nature.

For example, when I first began practicing listening prayer, I asked God, "Do you love me?" and "How much?" I will never forget what He showed me that day. Suddenly I was standing in the middle of a lush jungle, and in front of me was a massive waterfall. Then he spoke to me and said, "I love you with more power than all the water that ever has or ever will flow over this waterfall. That's how much I love you."

CREATION BLESSES US

I know this story may sound crazy to some, but I've experienced God's love through my crazy dog, Bailey. Last winter I got really sick with the flu as the result of a very stressful season of my life. I was so run down that when the flu got me, it hung on for dear life, and I was off work for a whole week. As I lay in my bed—lifeless, depressed, and in pain—my dog (a border collie who is usually off the wall) would jump up beside me. She'd come close to my face and sniff me with her little nose to make sure I was okay and then curl up beside me quietly. It was the simplest little thing but my dog, one of God's magnificent creatures, showed me His love. I've heard others express the way God's used a pet to bless them, and though it may seem strange, this is just one way He uses creation to bless us.

CREATION SUSTAINS US

Have you ever thought about how much we depend on all God created to sustain our everyday lives? If not for water, plants, and animals we physically couldn't live. (Well, some of you do just fine without meat, but you know what I mean!) Our existence is intertwined with the rest of creation, and through it God sustains us. Yet are we truly grateful for creation? Do we really treat it with the respect it deserves? And are we taking care of it the best way we can?

God's dream is for humanity and the rest of creation to be in unity. We are to rule over it (as He commanded in Genesis 1), but also to respect and appreciate it. As you go through your day today, don't take creation for granted. Let's remember the way it teaches us to worship, blesses us, and sustains us. Caring for it is the least we can do to show our gratitude to the Creator.

Dream Journal

1. What is your favorite part of creation?

2. What small lifestyle changes can you make to have a better "relationship" with God's creation?

3. Give a specific example of a time when creation taught you to worship, blessed you, or sustained you. What else has God given you through creation?

Meet the Dream-Giver

1. Imagine you are having lunch with Jesus. Take some time to express your gratitude to Him for the gift of his creation.

2. Ask Him what part of creation He would like to use to teach you something today.

BE HOLY

Day 6

"Be holy because I, the Lord your God, am holy."
(Leviticus 19:1)

Dream Manual: Read Hosea 1 and 2.
What would you do if God told you to marry a prostitute named Gomer? It's a strange question, I know, but the prophet Hosea was commanded to do just that, and he did. But why? Why would God ask a good and faithful man like Hosea to take an adulterous woman as his wife? What was the point?

The story of Hosea and Gomer is symbolic of our relationship with God. We are called to be "holy" as it says in Leviticus 10:1, but like Gomer we often "cheat" on God. We turn away from Him and choose to find the love and acceptance we desire everywhere else but from Him. We are like Gomer who *"went after her lovers, but me she forgot," declares the Lord"* (Hosea 2:13). Who or what are these other lovers? Anyone or anything we put in front of God in our lives is another lover or an idol. Anytime we devote more time or attention to our friends, our boyfriend/girlfriend, entertainment, sports, our "to-do lists," and so on, we turn our backs on God.

However, God's response, as modeled in the life of Hosea, shows *His* true character. Rather than letting us go our own destructive way, He chases after us and continues to pursue a relationship with us. Not only that, but He continues to call us to a higher way of living—a life of holiness. Check out this verse in Hosea 2:14: *"Therefore I am now going to allure her; I will lead her into the wilderness and speak tenderly to her."* Instead of throwing us away, He draws us back to Himself with His incredible love.

The Hebrew word for "holy" is *kadash* and it means "to set apart, to distinguish, to sanctify." This is God's big dream for humanity. He wants us to be a people who are unlike anyone else. He doesn't want us to walk around life going from "one lover to the next," trying to fill the empty void inside. He wants us to be set apart and distinguished. Not because of anything we've done ourselves, but because we have tasted a love that quenches our thirst and leaves us fully satisfied.

When I first graduated from high school, I started working full time to save money for bible school. At that time, a lot of the friends I made at work weren't Christians and spent most of their spare time partying, drinking, and hooking up with whomever they could find. When I asked one of my friends from work why she partied so much she told me it was the only way she could have fun, let go, and be herself. It broke my heart to hear her say those words because it showed just how empty she felt. Her life was all about trying to find something to fill the void inside of her, someone to love and accept her unconditionally. But instead of finding security in God, the one who longs to be the lover of her soul, she went to false lovers—just like Gomer did.

For some of you the problem isn't that you've been going to false lovers. Some of you have been treating God as though *He* was a false lover. How often do we say, "I want to be used by God"? What exactly does this expression mean? God doesn't want to just use you and leave you like a cheap prostitute. In fact, to view God this way means we don't really understand his love at all. What God wants more than to *use you* is to *know you*! Yet we often think if we aren't doing enough *for God* or we aren't being *used by Him* enough then He won't love us as much. The truth is that God is after your heart more than your service. He desires a deep and intimate relationship with you. God wants to know you and be known by you. The only way we can be holy is to pursue a love relationship with our Creator and allow His love to change us—to set us apart.

We need a change of perspective. Let's spend less time worshipping our idols and more time worshipping the one true God—the God who can fill all the empty spots in our hearts. Do you know that God is more than enough for you? He can fill your most intense and deepest desires, because He was the one to give you those desires in the first place! Do you feel a need for love and acceptance? Bring it to Him. A need for adventure and excitement? Bring it to Him. A need for peace and rest? Bring it to Him.

For those of us who think God wants us only for our service, it's time to let go of our pride. Remember that God is all-powerful, and He doesn't need you to get His work done. However, He does choose to allow us to be a part of His plan and in that way gives us significance and purpose. Maybe it's time to stop thinking of ourselves more highly than we ought to and humbly thank God for allowing us to be a part of His big dreams. Let's stop asking God to "use us" and instead ask to know Him more intimately than ever before. *"The fear of the Lord is the beginning of wisdom, and knowledge of the Holy One is understanding."* (Proverbs 9:10)

Dream Journal

1. In what ways have you "cheated" on God by putting other things in your life before Him?

2. Have you ever viewed God as someone who just wants to "use you"? Does it change your view of Him to think of working together with Him rather than being "used by Him"?

3. How can you be more faithful in your relationship with God this week?

Meet the Dream-Giver

1. Ask God where He would like to meet with you today.

2. In that place, ask Him to show you something new about Himself and how He feels about you right now.

Day 7

"Your kingdom come, your will be done, on earth as it is in heaven."
(Matthew 6:10)

Dream Manual: Read Matthew 6 and Luke 17:20–25.

When Jesus teaches the disciples to pray, He reveals what is most important to Him. He shows the disciples and the rest of us who now read His words what His big dream for the church is. One of the big dreams He reveals through the Lord's prayer is for us, the body of Christ, to usher the kingdom of heaven onto earth. But what does that mean? How are we supposed to bring God's kingdom to "earth as it is in heaven"?

The reality that surrounds us each and every day is temporary. The house you live in, the school you attend, the job you work, even the stuff you own—one day all of it will be gone. However, as followers of Christ we are a part of a different reality, an eternal reality. The moment you decided to give your life to Jesus, you began eternity with Him. No longer are we under the rule of sin. Instead we are under God's reign and a part of His kingdom. That is why, after teaching the disciples how to pray, Jesus encourages them not worry so much about their temporary reality (Matthew 6:25-34). He says, *"So do not worry, saying, 'What shall we eat?' or 'What shall we drink?' or 'What shall we wear?' For the pagans run after all these things, and your heavenly Father knows that you need them. But seek first his kingdom and his righteousness, and all these things will be given to you as well."* Our priority shouldn't be to build our earthly kingdoms but to usher in *His* eternal kingdom.

You have access to all the potential and power of heaven, God's kingdom, through the power of the Holy Spirit. Seeking His kingdom and righteousness first means choosing not to accept the temporary circumstances as your reality and instead ask God for what is true in heaven to be true here on earth. But what is true in heaven?

In Heaven:
- God is on the throne and Jesus is seated at His right hand (Ephesians 1:20)
- You are seated with Christ (Ephesians 2:6)
- There is no death, mourning, crying, or pain (Revelation 21:4)

Are you living in this reality each day? I know I'm not. It's easy to forget the authority we have because of what Christ did for us on the cross. It's easy to get bogged down in our current, temporary reality and forget we are not citizens of this fallen world, but citizens of heaven! Philippians 3:20–21 says, *"But our citizenship is in heaven. And we eagerly await a Savior from there, the Lord Jesus Christ, who, by the power that enables him to bring everything under his control, will transform our lowly bodies so that they will be like his glorious body."* The truth is that you are a member of God's kingdom and He wants you to bring the reality of that kingdom into your current situation.

Each and every day you have a choice: live under the reign of sin or usher in the kingdom of heaven. You have this choice because Jesus paid the price to give it to you. Because of His death and resurrection, you now have the *"keys of the kingdom of heaven; whatever you bind on earth will be bound in heaven, and whatever you loose on earth will be loosed in heaven"* (Matthew 16:19). That's pretty powerful stuff.

So when you are faced with an earthly, temporary reality that doesn't line up with the heavenly, eternal reality, don't accept it! Pray the prayer

Jesus modeled for us in Matthew, and ask for His kingdom to come and His will to be done on earth as it is in heaven. In heaven there is no need to worry, because we are seated with Christ at the right hand of the Father. In heaven there is no need to mourn, because death has lost its sting and victory. In heaven there is no crying or pain, because we are made whole and covered by God's amazing love.

Not only can you claim these heavenly truths for yourself, but for the people around you as well. This is what ushering in the kingdom means. It means bringing this reality to those around you who are suffering, who are hopeless, who are in pain. It means sharing the hope of heaven with others instead of keeping it for ourselves.

Matthew 13:47 says, *"Once again, the kingdom of heaven is like a net that was let down into the lake and caught all kinds of fish."* The kingdom is supposed to be ever-expanding—reaching out to a world in need. As carriers of the kingdom, it is our job to be like this net, catching all kinds of people and drawing them into something greater than the here and now. How far is your net reaching? Who will be brought into the kingdom of heaven because of you and your willingness to bring the reality of heaven onto earth?

Dream Journal

1. What is one area of your life in which you need to ask for the kingdom to come on earth as it is in heaven?

2. What does it mean to you that God has given you the *"keys to the kingdom of heaven"*?

3. How can you share the reality of God's kingdom with someone in your life this week? (Be specific about who and how.)

Meet the Dream-Giver

1. Imagine you were to meet Jesus in heaven today. Where would He be?

2. How would you approach Him, and how would He respond?

3. What would He say to you?

Day 8

"All the believers were one in heart and mind." (Acts 4:32)

Dream Manual: Read Acts 4:32–37 and Ephesians 4:1–16.

What does it mean to live in community with others, and why is this one of Jesus' big dreams for His children, the church? The English definition of the word "community" is simply "with unity." Jesus desires us to live in unity with other believers. The Greek definition of the word "unity" (Greek is the original language of the New Testament) is "agreement, alike, common and one." Ephesians 4:3 says, *"Make every effort to keep the unity of the Spirit through the bond of peace."* In this passage, Paul expresses the importance of unity to the body of believers he is writing to, the church in Ephesus. It's clear from the wording of this text that Paul understands the challenge of remaining unified, because he acknowledges that it will take effort to do so, but he says that we *should* make the effort.

But doing life with others is hard. It's much easier to do what we feel like doing when we feel like doing it. It's much more convenient to plan our lives around our individual wants and desires, rather than considering how our decisions affect others. If you've ever had to live in a community setting, you know how true this statement is.

One of my first experiences of the challenge of living in community occurred the year after I graduated from high school. I decided to attend Capernwray Bible School in New Zealand, and for five months I lived, learned, and worked with a small group of about 40 other young adults. The day I arrived in Auckland, New Zealand, I met a few girls at the hostel who would also be attending the school, and one of them just rubbed me the wrong way. From the moment we met I could tell we had little in common, and for some reason she just annoyed me. The day we arrived on campus, I was assigned to my room and went to drop off my luggage. As I was in the bathroom, I prayed to God that this girl wouldn't be my roommate. But as I prayed those selfish words, somehow I knew I was about to eat them. Sure enough, when I stepped out of the bathroom, that very girl walked in to my room and dropped her stuff on the top bunk of my bed. At first, everything she did drove me crazy and I wondered why God stuck me with the one person I wanted to avoid. But slowly I began to pray for her and ask God to give me His love and heart for her, and in the end we became friends. I soon realized that a lot of the things that annoyed me were character traits I possessed as well (being strong-willed, a leader, and not afraid to speak my mind). As I learned to see her through God's eyes, He used our friendship to teach me about true community.

Have you ever had an experience like this where living in community was tough? Maybe it was in your youth group, at school, or on a sports team. How did you respond? If you're anything like me, you likely tried to avoid the person or people who rubbed you the wrong way. But if we are to live the big dream Jesus has for us, we need to pursue unity and make every effort to work with these difficult people rather than avoid them. But how? Here are three easy ways to work to build up the community you are a part of.

BE HUMBLE, GENTLE, AND PATIENT

Being humble means considering others more important than ourselves. Who are the people in your life you haven't been treating with humility? Maybe they're your parents or your brothers and sisters. Perhaps it's that person you work with whom everyone makes fun of and dislikes. God calls us to treat those people with gentleness and patience. This means instead of getting annoyed and avoiding them, we go out of our way to be kind and have patience even when doing so is tough. This is our call as believers of Christ! It's not to take the path of least resistance, to be just like everyone else, but to go the opposite way of the crowd. When we treat others as though they are better than ourselves, we show those people—and the world that's watching—who Jesus is and what His love is like.

FIND COMMON GROUND
When God puts someone new in your path, make an effort to find common ground with that person. Perhaps all you can see are the differences you may have, but rather than focusing on those and allowing them to divide you, why not make it your goal to look for similarities? Perhaps you have the same taste in music, food, or extracurricular activities. Maybe you come from similar family situations or you've both gone through the same challenging experience. The only way to find common ground is to ask questions and truly listen. You may be amazed at how much you have in common, and when you focus on this goal as your starting point, unity is a whole lot easier to find and maintain.

LOOK FOR AND ENCOURAGE EACH OTHER'S UNIQUE GIFTS
Our gifts weren't given to us so we could be a "one man show," impressing the world and God with how amazing we are. Our gifts work best when they are used within a community setting in cooperation with the gifts of those around us. We are designed to be one piece of the puzzle, not the whole picture. Think about how your gifts can be used to build up the community God has placed you in. And when you notice strengths in others, tell them what you've noticed. Encourage them to do the same for others. I've often found the best way to get more connected in a community, especially a church community, is to use the gifts God has given me to serve others. When we do so, we fulfill the dream Jesus has for the church—true unity.

Dream Journal

1. What has your experience of Christian community been like?

2. How can you improve your contributions to your community?

3. Why do you think community is important to Jesus? Why is it better than people living, working, and serving Him on their own?

Meet the Dream-Giver

1. Ask Jesus to bring to mind one or two people from your current community with whom He wants you to find common ground. Write down their names and all the things you may have in common with them.

2. Pray for these people, and ask God to give you His eyes to see them.

Day 9

"Instead, speaking the truth in love, we will in all things grow up into him who is the Head, that is, Christ." (Ephesians 4:15)

Dream Manual: Read Romans 12:1–8.

One of the biggest mistakes I see youth and young adults making as they pursue their big dreams, is trying to do so on their own without support and accountability. One of Jesus' dreams for the church was for us to be unified, working together to accomplish *His* purposes here on earth. We are not meant to walk this path alone. We talked a bit about this yesterday, but today I want to look more specifically at the importance of accountability and mentorship.

A close friend of mine once said that God brings people into our lives for "a reason, a season, or a lifetime." For me, mentorship relationships have always been for "a season." I've had many amazing mentors over the years and learned a great deal from each one of them. These relationships were usually formed in church through my involvement in youth group and through volunteering in different ministry areas. Through each of these friendships I learned from the example set by my mentors as well as their words of encouragement and sometimes correction. Have you ever had a mentor? Do you have one now?

A mentor is someone who is older, more mature, and usually further along in his or her journey with Christ than you are. A mentor is someone you respect and want to be like in some way. If you don't have someone like this, I encourage you to ask God for one and to actively look for a person who could be your mentor. Not only can mentors encourage you, but they can also provide good advice and wise counsel as you pursue your relationship with God and the big dreams He has planted in your heart. They can also give you a kick in the butt when you need it, and we all do sometimes!

Another important relationship to pursue is an accountability partner. This could be your mentor, or it could be a peer—someone who is at a similar place in his or her journey and possibly even working towards similar goals. If a mentor is like your coach as you train for a marathon, an accountability partner is like your running buddy—someone to keep you going when you want to give in and vice versa. What's the difference between an accountability partner and a best friend, you might ask. It's all about "intentionality." You may have an amazing best friend already, but how often do you talk about the things that really matter to you? How much time do you spend making goals together and checking up on how the pursuit of those goals is going? How often do you pray together? And how often do you speak the hard truth to one another in a loving and kind way? If you're already doing these things, then your best friend is the perfect accountability partner! And if you're not, maybe you could in the future.

A few weeks ago one of my accountability partners (who also happens to be a close friend) did just that for me. She challenged me about something I'd done and gently let me know she thought it was wrong. As hard as it was to hear those words, I appreciated her honesty, because without this kind of honest correction, I won't improve and grow. I'm far from perfect, and sometimes I need someone to remind me of this fact and challenge me to live and love better.

In many ways it is much easier not to have a mentor or accountability partner in our lives. But the only way you can really see your big dreams come to pass is to have people around you who will speak the truth in love to you. It's not about criticizing you or putting you down for your faults either. It's about someone believing that God has called you to a higher standard, a better way, and encouraging and challenging you to live that way. Allowing a trusted friend to call you higher and push you to be more of the person God has created you to be is invaluable.

If you don't already have a mentor or accountability partner, think and pray this week about who that person could be. If you do have one already, why not ask that person how he or she thinks you can continue to grow and improve, even if the answer may be hard for you to hear.

Dream Journal

1. Describe one person who is or could be your accountability partner. What are the character traits you are looking for in this type of person?

2. If you asked this person to describe your strengths and weaknesses, what do you think would be the answer?

3. What is one area of your life you'd like to grow in, and how can you get help from an accountability partner or mentor in order to do so?

Meet the Dream-Giver

1. Ask God who He'd like to have mentor you. List the names He brings to mind.

2. Perhaps it's time for you to be a mentor to someone else. Pray about this topic, and see what Jesus thinks about it. Who would He have you mentor or offer accountability to?

Look After Orphans and Widows

Day 10

"Blessed is he who has regard for the weak; the Lord delivers him in times of trouble." (Psalms 41:1)

Dream Manual: Read Matthew 25:34–40 and James 1:27.

As I was checking my e-mail one Wednesday afternoon, I noticed a message from an old friend in my inbox. I clicked on it curiously, as I'd never received an email from her before and couldn't imagine why she would be writing. It was a request to speak at a downtown drop-in centre for kids in the north end, the poorest area of Winnipeg. I gave her a call to ask for more details. She told me it was an event for teen girls and asked if I could speak about true beauty and identity in Christ. We discussed the when and where, and then she told me that they wouldn't be able to pay me for speaking. Now I'm all for volunteering my time, but I had recently quit my full-time teaching job and was depending on speaking and writing for my income. However, I felt that this was a great opportunity and told her I'd love to help out.

After we got off the phone, I found myself feeling frustrated that I was being asked to volunteer as a speaker once again. The last four events I'd been asked to speak at were also volunteer opportunities. I was beginning to feel like I'd never get anywhere financially and would end up going back to full-time teaching. As all these thoughts rolled around in my head, I sat down and opened my Bible to the Psalm of the day. (I like to read one Psalm and one Proverb per day.) It said this: *"Blessed is he who has regard for the weak; the Lord delivers him in times of trouble"* (Psalm 41:1). Wow! Could God speak any more clearly? Here I was worrying about how I was going to pay the bills if I kept giving away my time, and the truth was that giving away my time was the solution. Jesus has such a heart for the weak that He promises when we look out for them He will look out for us. I assume the opposite is true as well. When we go about chasing after our dreams and have no regard for the weak, the Lord may not deliver us in our own times of trouble.

I'd like to look a little deeper into this truth that is so clearly one of Jesus' big dreams for the world, but first let's define the word "weak." In the example I gave earlier, the weak were girls who were financially and socially less fortunate. But the weak can be any of us. Weakness can be physical, emotional, mental, or spiritual; it can relate to race, age, gender, or social class. When Jesus walked the earth, He specifically commanded us to look out for people who were at any kind of disadvantage. I think it is safe to say that the weak includes anyone who has a need that we have the ability to fill. Check out these verses from Matthew 25:35-36:

"For I was hungry (need) and you gave me something to eat (fill the need),
I was thirsty (need) and you gave me something to drink (fill the need),
I was a stranger (need) and you invited me in (fill the need),
I needed clothes (need) and you clothed me (fill the need),
I was sick (need) and you looked after me (fill the need),
I was in prison (need) and you came to visit me (fill the need)."

It's not rocket science, right? If we want to fulfill Jesus' big dream for the world, we just have to look for a need and fill it. Find those who are weak in some way, and help them out. But don't think that we do this for an ego-boost. Helping the "weak" doesn't mean that we are somehow better or stronger or more spiritual than them; quite the opposite, in fact. 1 Corinthians 1:27 says, *"God chose the foolish things of the world to shame the wise; God chose the weak things of the world to shame the strong."* This verse suggests that the real reason God wants us to help the weak is so that we can *learn* from them! God uses the weak to shame the strong, not the other way around. He wants us to be around the weak for our own good, not for theirs.

So often North Americans want to go to third world countries to help people because they have such an obvious need for basic necessities like food, water, and shelter. But it is dangerous to think we should go somewhere like Haiti or Thailand because these people desperately *need* us to fix their lives. The reality is that we should go not primarily to fix or change them but to learn from them. Yes, we have a lot to offer in terms of finances, food, clothing, etc., but they may have even more to offer us. Perhaps they are the ones God has chosen to use like the verse says—*"the foolish to shame the wise, the weak to shame the strong."*

My final thought on this aspect of Jesus' heart for the world is that because Jesus loves the weak, we should feel free to be honest about our own weakness to Him and to others. Being polished, put together, and perfect is not the best way to see our dreams come true. In 2 Corinthians 12:10, we read, *"My grace is sufficient for you, for my power is made perfect in weakness. Therefore I will boast all the more gladly about my weakness, so that Christ's power may rest on me."* This verse proves that we don't need to be strong in order to be used by God in incredible ways. We can come to Him just as we are—broken, confused, afraid—and by His grace He will empower us to do mighty things in His kingdom.

Dream Journal

1. What is one area in your life where you are weak?

2. Write out a short prayer asking God for His power to be perfect through this weakness.

3. Fill in the chart with information about three people you know with needs you have the ability to fill.

NAME	NEED	HOW YOU CAN FILL THE NEED

Meet the Dream-Giver

1. Ask Jesus to show you what needs of yours He would like to meet today.

2. If you were to bring one person to Jesus today, who would it be and how would He want to help them?

Day 11

"*Therefore go and make disciples of all nations, baptizing them in the name of the Father and of the Son and of the Holy Spirit and teaching them to obey everything I have commanded you.*" (Matthew 28:19–20)

Dream Manual: Read 1 Corinthians 9:19–23.

What if the person you loved most passed away, and the last thing this person asked—a dying wish—was for you to sell the thing you loved most and give the money to charity? Would you do it? What if this person asked you to sell all of your favorite things and give the money away? What if this person asked you to give away everything you own and move to the jungles of Ecuador to be a missionary? Would you do it then?

Jesus' last words to His friends on earth were, "*Therefore go and make disciples.*" It was a command to leave behind one way of living and actively move into another. Many Christians interpret this verse as a command to physically "go" somewhere else other than the place they are from (e.g., become a missionary in Africa or Asia). However, the Greek word "go" is more accurately translated "as you go." It is a command to adopt a new lifestyle—one where even *as you go* about your day-to-day routine you are making disciples. How does one make disciples, you might be wondering? Well, how did Jesus do it? He didn't move across the planet. He found people right in his own neighborhood and became friends with them. *"As Jesus was walking beside the Sea of Galilee, he saw two brothers… 'Come follow me, and I will make you fishers of men.' At once they left their nets and followed him"* (Matthew 3:18–19). Jesus was just out for a walk and started a conversation—a strange one, yes, but just a conversation with two guys He ran into. As He went about his everyday life He saw people, started conversations, and invited them into a different way of living. We are called to do the same.

Is your life one that makes people want to be followers of Christ? Are you teaching others to obey everything Jesus has taught you? Are you a "go-er"? If not, you're missing out on one of the big dreams that Jesus has for you. He wants your life to be about sharing His love and grace with others! He doesn't want you to stay within the comfort of the four walls of your church, the safety of your clique at school, the security of your family. He wants you to walk out the door and right into the lives of the people that you meet along the way.

- Do you really see the person that sits beside or behind you in class?
- Have you ever asked that person what his or her story is?
- Do you talk to the lonely-looking person you meet at the bus stop?
- Have you ever helped someone in need, even if it means changing your plans?

I'm not talking about moving to the jungles of South America here, people! I'm talking about opening your eyes and really seeing the people that are right in front of you each and every day. Seeing them and being bold enough to both demonstrate and speak the love of Christ to them. That's what Jesus did. He didn't just show people through His actions— He also spoke boldly and creatively to draw people into conversation and cause them to think and ask questions. Jesus' dream is that we as the church do the same!

Although the command "go" doesn't always mean moving to a different geographical location, sometimes it does. Some of you reading this book are called to overseas missions. Some of you are called to move to a different city in North America to share God's love. Some of you are called to move to a different area of your own city to reach those in need. And ALL of us are called to share God's love with the people God puts in our paths, each and every day.

What would it look like if believers lived in such a way that "as they went" they made disciples? I imagine the church would grow by leaps and bounds, but I also think we would see God do amazing things. Just look at the lives of the disciples, the ones who were first given this command and actually obeyed it whole-heartedly. Peter, for example, would just walk past a sick person and his shadow would bring healing! (Check out Acts 4:12–16.)

How is it possible to live this kind of life? It sounds radical, doesn't it? Well, the only way that it's possible is because of the word "therefore." Look back at the verse we started with today. What's the first word you see? "Therefore." This word basically means, "STOP! Look at what I just said!" Let's do that. In the verse directly before the command to "go," Jesus says, *"All authority in heaven and on earth has been given to me."* These words are meant to remind us that Jesus did everything He did through the supernatural power God gave Him; through the Holy Spirit, we have access to that power as well. It is only through the power of the Holy Spirit that we can truly obey the command to "go and make disciples." Without that power we can do nothing, but with it we can see lives changed, sickness healed, and God glorified. Let's end today with this verse: *"The Spirit of him who raised Jesus from the dead is living in you"* (Romans 8:11). We have access to the one who raised Christ from the dead, and only *through His power* we can live out Jesus' big dream to "go and make disciples."

Dream Journal

1. What is the difference between "go" and "as you go"?

2. Describe one part of your daily/weekly routine where you could become more aware of the people around you and share God's love with them.

3. Have you ever had the opportunity to share God's love with someone other than family or friends? What was it like to do that?

4. What does it teach you about Jesus that His big dream for us is to "go and make disciples"?

Meet the Dream-Giver
1. Ask Jesus who He wants you to pray for today.

2. Imagine yourself bringing that person to Jesus in your secret place. What would He do/say to them?

PART TWO

GOD'S DREAM
FOR
You

THE DREAM-GIVER'S VOICE

Day 12

"The man who enters by the gate is the shepherd of his sheep. The watchman opens the gate for him, and the sheep listen to his voice. He calls his own sheep by name and leads them out…His sheep follow him because they know his voice." (John 10:4)

Dream Manual: Read 1 Samuel 3.

Do you know that God has a big dream specifically for your life? He truly has something planned for you beyond all you could ask or imagine. We've spent the past 11 days defining some of God's big dreams for humanity by looking at the story of Israel in the Old Testament and the life of Jesus in the New Testament. Now it's time to talk about God's big dream for *you*. In order to define God's dream for you, it is essential to learn how to hear God's voice directly. How else can you know what His dream for you is? He wants to tell you about it. Now you may be thinking, "I've had to listen to all of God's dreams for the last 11 days. Let's get on with what I want!" But that's not really how it works. In fact, if you were to try and come up with a big dream apart from God's plan, it wouldn't really be that big, would it?

Recently I spent some time at a writing conference, and the entire time people were telling me that getting a book published is next to impossible. The experts all say that only .01% of all manuscripts submitted are actually published. Initially I felt really discouraged by this information. However, as I thought about it more I sensed God whisper to me, "I want to do the impossible in your life!" That's what I want too. Don't you want to see such wild and amazing things happen in your life that people will look at them and say, "That could only be God!" Here is a verse that says it best: *"With man this is impossible, but with God all things are possible"* (Matt. 19:26).

So what is the big dream—the impossible thing God wants to do in and through your life? Don't ask me. Ask God! He wants to speak to you about His plans for your life. The story you read today from 1 Samuel 3 describes the supernatural way God can speak to us and make His plans clear. Samuel was just a kid when God first called him. The passage says that Samuel was sleeping when he heard a voice say his name. At first he thought it was his master's voice, but when he asked, Eli said he hadn't called and sent Samuel back to bed. Samuel heard the voice a second time and again mistakenly thought it was Eli. Why didn't he know it was God? Verse 7 says, *"Now Samuel did not yet know the Lord: The word of the Lord had not yet been revealed to him."* We as Christians actually have a one-up on Samuel! The word of the Lord has been revealed to us through the persons of Jesus Christ and the Holy Spirit. John 1:1 confirms this truth, saying, *"The word became flesh and made his dwelling among us."* Because Jesus came, we have the ability to hear and recognize the voice of God speaking directly to us.

If we have the ability to recognize God's voice, why don't we? Why does it so often feel like God's plan for us is a mystery? One reason: we don't spend enough time listening! So often we treat God like an answering service. We call Him up, tell Him our problems, give our requests, vent our anger, and then hang up before giving Him a chance to respond. How do we expect to hear God's voice if we never stop and listen for it? How can He give us the answers we are seeking if we don't even ask Him our questions and wait to hear from Him?

A few years ago I was trying to decide what to do for a summer job.

I had the choice to work as a counselor at a camp in British Colombia or go on six-week speaking tour. At first I wanted to go to the camp in BC more than the tour and I felt like there wasn't a "right" or "wrong" decision. However, I wanted God's direction and His big dream for my summer, so I prayed and asked Him where He wanted me to go. The next week I had three distinct dreams, and in each one I was traveling in some sort of vehicle. (Vehicles in dreams often represent life direction.) In each dream I was trying to get somewhere in the vehicle, but each time I didn't make it. In one, my car got squashed by a fallen tree, in another I raced around a track endlessly, and in the third, I was in an accident. I realized that these dreams were God speaking to me about the camp in BC I was planning to go to. Because of those dreams, I turned down the job. I later found out that my ex-boyfriend and his new girlfriend (that I didn't know about) were working at the camp in BC. If I had gone there, it would have been a long and difficult summer. And instead I ended up going on the six-week tour where I met my husband! Looking back, I'm so glad I asked God for His plan and listened for His answer. It came in a way I didn't expect, but because I listened and waited, I heard from Him.

Dream Journal

1. What's one new thing you've learned about God through the verses in Matthew and 1 Samuel?

2. Describe a time when you felt you heard God's voice.

3. In your prayer life, do you treat God more like an answering service or a two-way phone call? Why?

4. If you could ask God one question right now, what would it be and why?

5. How would you feel if God called you in the night like He did to Samuel?

Meet the Dream-Giver

1. Look back on your life, and ask God to show you a time when He spoke to you. Describe what happened.

2. Ask God the questions you wrote for #4, and listen for His answer, believing that He really does want to speak directly to you.

3. If you were to meet with God today, where would it be and why?

4. If He were to give you a gift related to your future and his dream for you, what would it be? Why?

Day 13

"For I know the plans I have for you', declares the Lord, 'plans to prosper you and not to harm you, plans to give you hope and a future'." (Jeremiah 29:11)

Dream Manual: Read Ephesians 2:1–10.

God has a unique and incredible plan for your life. He has something for you to accomplish that no one else on the face of the planet can do the way you can. If you don't live this dream out, who will? Ephesians 2:10 says, *"For we are God's workmanship, created in Christ Jesus to do good works, which God prepared in advance for us to do."* This verse tells us two things. First, when God created you it was a purposeful act. You are not an accident. Second, the purpose He prepared for you is to "do good works." Well, that's a little vague, isn't it? Wouldn't it be nice if the Scripture said He prepared you to "be a doctor" or to "be a singer and songwriter"? It's hard to define God's unique dream for you based on one verse alone, which is why you need to hear from God directly.

Maybe you already have a pretty clear idea of what your big dream is. Or maybe you have no clue. Either way, today is all about getting a clearer picture from God about His dream for you. It's even possible that some of the things you really want aren't exactly what God wants for you. I know you probably don't like the sound of that, but let me explain a bit more.

The day I realized God's dream for my life was July 20th, 2002. I was traveling in Australia after completing five months of Bible school in New Zealand. It was Sunday morning, and my travel buddies and I were looking for a church in the small town of Byron Bay. We picked one out of the phone book and showed up, not knowing a soul. Right away the pastor greeted us and, after hearing briefly about where we were coming from, asked if one of us would share about our time at Bible school. My two friends quickly volunteered me, and I accepted.

When I got up to share, I felt calm and was able to speak clearly about what God was doing in my life. Even though I didn't know a single person standing in front of me, I wasn't nervous or afraid. After the service was over, the pastor came and prayed for me, and then it happened. He looked straight into my eyes and said, "Heather, you were born to be a preacher. Don't stop until you're speaking in front of thousands." Those words were a new beginning for me—the birth of God's unique dream for my life. But as I said earlier, sometimes what we think we want doesn't always happen the way we think it should, or when we think it should.

I didn't speak again until three years after that day in Australia, and when I did I quickly became caught up in the idea of being successful and well-known. Instead of focusing on bringing glory to God, the one I was speaking about, I wanted the glory for myself. I wanted success. I wanted influence. My dream went off course and became something different from what God originally intended. It became all about me and not about Him.

What about you? What are the things you want most in life? The world says the BIG DREAMS are fame and fortune, money and comfort, power and popularity. Are your current dreams more in line with the world's, or is there still room for God's way in your heart? It may look different than you think it should, but it will always be the best way.

Defining God's dream is a process, and it may not happen today. In fact, I'm sure it will take longer than that. But here are a few things you can do today to get a little closer to knowing what His dream for your life is:

1. Write down a list of all the things you want to accomplish in your life.
2. Look at this list and see if any of your dreams clearly line up with God's dreams for humanity and Jesus' dreams for the church (the ones we studied in Day 1–11).
3. Look at the list again, and see if any of your dreams line up more with the world's big dreams (money, fame, popularity, power, etc.).
4. Spend some time in listening prayer, and ask God to highlight a few things on your list that *He* wants for your life—things He's really gifted you to do. Which ones stand out the most after taking this time to pray? (This may mean adding a new idea or crossing one off.)

At the end of the day, God truly wants what's best for you. He has plans to prosper you, to give you hope and a future. He is good and has good things for you to do. But also know He sees the bigger picture—your beginning, present, and eternity—and His perspective on "the best" may be different from yours. Sometimes what is good is not fun or easy. "Good for you" like broccoli, not "good" like chocolate. Know what I mean? *"For my thoughts are not your thoughts, neither are your ways, my ways', declares the Lord"* (Isaiah 55:8). This is a good thing. Take comfort in knowing the one who holds the universe in His hands sees, knows, and loves you incredibly. His plan and dream for you is truly the best there is, and it's worth seeking above all else!

Dream Journal and Meet the Dream-Giver
Do the four steps from today's lesson as your journaling and listening prayer time.

Day 14

"Commit to the Lord whatever you do, and your plans will succeed."
(Proverbs 16:3)

Dream Manual: Read 2 Corinthians 5:1–10.

The lessons for today and tomorrow are all about practical steps you can take to pursue the big dreams God has given you. Today you are going to take some time to make a list of your five-year goals and some practical steps you can take in order to move toward those goals. I'm also going to give you a ton of verses to look up that demonstrate how much God wants to be a part of both goal-setting and goal-accomplishing in your life.

First of all, I want to you look back at yesterday's lesson and remind yourself of the things God spoke to you about His unique dream for your life. What are some of the strengths and gifts He has given you? What visions did He show you for your future? If the answer still feels very unclear, go back to yesterday's lesson; spend some more time in listening prayer, and wait to complete today's lesson.

Time to start your list. Feel free to fill in the chart below or write it in your journal or on a separate piece of paper. I've left room for three main goals in each category, but feel free to write more if you'd like. I've also given an example for each section; these happen to be a few of my personal goals. Here are some questions to think about as you work:

- Where do you see yourself in five years?
- Where do you hope to be spiritually, vocationally, relationally, and even physically?
- What things have you always wanted to do but never thought were possible?

God cares about every detail of your life and wants to be a part of the planning process. And don't think this work is only limited to spiritual goals. Feel free to include any and all of the things you'd like to accomplish, including places you'd like to go, things you'd like to do, etc. Say a prayer before you begin, and ask God to direct your thoughts as you plan.

FIVE-YEAR GOALS

SPIRITUAL GOALS eg. *Memorize the book of James* 1. 2. 3.	EDUCATIONAL/ VOCATIONAL GOALS eg. *Finish my first book* 1. 2. 3.
RELATIONAL GOALS (friends and family) eg. *Find a spiritual mother/mentor* 1. 2. 3.	PHYSICAL/ HEALTH GOALS eg. *Run the 1/2 marathon* 1. 2. 3.
TRAVEL GOALS eg. *Travel to Thailand, Africa or India* 1. 2. 3.	JUST FOR FUN GOALS eg. *Try bungee-jumping* 1. 2. 3.

(Check out www.heatherboersma.com for "Five Year Goals" worksheet you can print out for free.)

If God were to make a list for you do you think it would be similar to yours? Take a moment to ask Him if there is anything on your list He would like to add or change. Remember this truth as you do that: *"For I know the plans I have for you', declares the Lord. 'Plans to prosper you and not to harm you, plans to give you hope and a future'"* (Jeremiah 29:11). Goal-setting is an activity we as followers of Christ should always do *with* God. Ultimately His plans are the best, and if we can line ours up with His they will give us hope and a future.

As you look at this list, how would you feel if God's plans were completely different and none of your goals would come true? If you've been listening to His voice and making your goals based on God's dreams for humanity and Jesus' dreams for the church that you learned about in Days 1–10, then that likely will not happen. But what if it did? Would you still trust God? Would you still want His plan more than your own? *"In his heart a man plans his course, but the Lord determines his steps"* (Proverbs 16:9). At the end of the day, I would rather have God, who can see the beginning, middle, and end of the story, plan my steps than do so on my own. If that means I end up in a different place five years from now than I originally planned, it's okay. It will be the best place for me and for God to use me to build His kingdom. Make sure you keep your Five-Year Goal list open to God to adjust as He sees fit.

The last thing I want you to do with this list is show it to a mentor, leader, or a friend you respect spiritually. Ask for feedback and advice. Is there anything this person would add or change? Why should you take this step? Because the Bible recommends it: *"Make plans by seeking advice, if you wage war, obtain guidance"* (Proverbs 20:18). We were not meant to make this journey on our own. God has placed people in our lives who can give us advice, and this is one of the areas where you should seek that help. Not only can advisors point out plans that might need redirecting, but they can also pray for you, encourage you, and hold you accountable to taking steps towards the dreams you are pursuing.

Dream Journal

1. Which goal on your Five-Year Goal list seems almost impossible to accomplish? Why?

2. How does Mark 10:27 encourage you as you work toward this goal?

3. What things may stand in your way as you work toward accomplishing these goals?

Meet the Dream-Giver

1. Ask God if there is anything on your list that He doesn't want there or anything you may have missed.

2. Ask Jesus, "When you look at my list, what is one word that comes to your mind?" You may be surprised at what He says!

Day 15

"*Many are the plans in a person's heart, but it is the Lord's purpose that prevails.*" (Proverbs 19:21)

Dream Manual: Read Proverbs 16.

Yesterday we looked at creating five-year goals, which could be considered "long-term goals." Today we're going to make the process even more practical by taking those long-term goals and breaking them down into one-year or "short-term goals." This is where your plans start to get real, because by the end of today you should have a list of steps you can take this month to get you closer to your end goal. This work is exciting, but it's also a bit scary, because it may be the first time in your journey toward your dream where you experience failure. It's easy enough to dream about a path you would like to take, but only when you start walking down that path do you realize how steep or twisting or difficult the road might be. However, if you don't start moving forward, you'll never get where you're trying to go.

Find hope in these words from Isaiah 30:21: "*Whether you turn to the right or to the left, your ears will hear a voice behind you, saying, 'This is the way; walk in it.*'" As long as we are listening to the voice of our

Shepherd, He will direct our steps. Why not take a moment and ask God to help you come up with your one-year goals right now, before we go any further? Perhaps you could pray something like this: "God, I love you, and I want to honor you with my life. Please help me to take my big dreams and break them down into pracitcal steps I can take this month. And remind me that my ultimate goal is to know you more each day. Amen."

Now that we've committed this time to the Lord, let's get right to work. Go back to yesterday's lesson, and review the goals you wrote down. Actually do it! It's just a few pages back. Maybe as you look over the list you realize there was something you forgot or you'd like to change. Make those changes now so that the steps you plan out today can be as purposeful and direct as possible.

Next, choose one of your long-term goals to use as an example, and write it down in the space below. Beneath the long-term goal, write down two or three short-term goals you think can be accomplished in the next year. For example, your long-term goal might be to become a doctor. What are a few short-term goals you can set for this year that will get you closer to that end goal? You'll probably need to take (and pass!) several university courses, start volunteering at the local hospital, and maybe meet with a practicing doctor who can give you some advice. Your three short-term goals should be things you can actually achieve in a year.

Long-Term Goal:

1. _____

Short-Term Goals:

1. _____
2. _____
3. _____

After you've finished with your long- and short-term goals, it's time to break the steps down even more. Have a look at your short term goals, and think about what steps you'll need to take each month to accomplish your short-term goals by the end of the year. Using the doctor example again, perhaps this month you can go online and look up the requirements you'll need to get into the university program you'll be taking. Or maybe next month you can call the local hospital and find out if it needs volunteers. Try to come up with one step for each month of the next year that will directly help you accomplish one of your short-term goals. This kind of planning is how we make our dreams practical and attainable.

Monthly Steps:

January:	July:
February:	August:
March:	September:
April:	October:
May:	November:
June:	December:

Dream Journal

Use this time today to fill out your long and short-term goals as well as your monthly steps.

Meet the Dream-Giver

1. Take some time to commit your plans to Jesus in prayer.

2. Imagine yourself bringing the list of your steps to Him. What would He do with it? How would He respond to you?

Day 16

"*His master replied, 'Well done, good and faithful servant! You have been faithful with a few things; I will put you in charge of many things.'*" (Matthew 25:23)

Dream Manual: Read Matthew 25:14–46.

I was driving home from a long day of work, exhausted from being on my feet for eight hours. Singing along to the radio, I stopped behind a line of traffic at the three-way stop just a few blocks from home. Gazing out the passenger window, I noticed a girl sitting on the bus stop bench. She looked about 18 years old, wore dark make-up, and had her long, black hair pulled into a ponytail. What stood out to me the most wasn't her appearance but that she was crying. More like sobbing actually. Mascara streamed down her pale cheeks, and it struck me. I couldn't look away and felt the sudden urge to pull over and talk to her. In fact, it was as though God was tapping me on the shoulder and telling me to go talk to her.

"Pull over the car, Heather. Go ask her what's wrong."

"Are you crazy, Lord? I don't even know her. She'll think I'm nuts."

"Pull over, Heather."

I found myself turning the corner after the stop sign, pulling over, and opening the car door. As I walked towards her, fear and doubt swarmed my head like annoying black flies, the ones that follow you on long summer walks, driving you crazy and making you want to turn back. But I didn't. Instead I walked right up to her, sat down, and asked her if she was okay. She spent the next few minutes telling me how she had just been fired from her job and had no bus fare to get home. I offered her a ride, which she declined, and instead I give her some money for the bus. I asked her if I could pray for her, and she shook her head, tears falling into open hands. I told her I would pray for her, and she thanked me. I walked away with my heart racing, wishing there was more I could have done. Talking to her felt like a small thing, but it was the small thing God asked me to do that day.

When God plants His dreams in us, we often have to wait to see them fulfilled. However, this doesn't mean we sit around watching TV, checking Facebook, and waiting for our big dreams to come knocking. There are little opportunities every day, like the girl crying at the bus stop, that God uses to prepare us for our big dreams. If only we weren't so easily distracted.

Check out these stats on how teens, aged 12–18, spend their time on an average day:
- 4 ½ hours watching TV
- 2 ½ hours listening to music
- 1 ½ hours on the computer
- 1 ¼ hours playing video games
- 25 minutes watching movies

Total media use per day = Approx. 10 hours! (More than you spend in school or sleeping!!)

This is what I call distraction. Satan uses distraction to get us away from pursuing and living our big dream. He doesn't want us to go out into the world and accomplish God's purposes. We are much less of a threat to him when we are distracted from our dreams. In fact, we could waste away our whole lives on distraction, but would we be satisfied? How many of you want to be remembered for how well you played video games? Or how good you were at updating your Facebook status every 10 minutes? I know I don't want my tombstone to read: "Heather Boersma–A great TV watcher!"

So how do we keep from wasting our lives on distraction? How can we have our eyes open to see the little opportunities God is giving us to be "faithful with a few"? We need to start looking at our present circumstances—the little things God has put in front of us—and treat them as though they are our big dreams. Your school, friends, family, and job are all things God asks you to be faithful with. Treat these things with as much importance as if they were your ultimate goals, and eventually God promises He will "put you in charge of many things." And as you go through your day, don't allow distraction to steal you away from the present—the people right in front of you, such as the girl crying at the bus stop. You never know how God may use these situations to prepare for the next step in your journey with Him.

Dream Journal

1. In the Parable of the Talents why is the master unhappy with the servant who buried the treasure?

2. What gifts do you feel God has given you?

3. What are you presently doing to invest those gifts into the kingdom of God?

4. What things are distracting you from seeing the little opportunities God may be giving you to be "faithful with a few"?

5. What is one way you can be faithful with something God has put in your life (a person, an opportunity, a habit) this week?

Meet the Dream-Giver

1. Imagine yourself in your secret place with Jesus. Ask Him what gift He would like to give you today.

2. Why does He want to give you that particular gift?

3. How can you use the gift He's given you to work towards your big dream?

4. Ask Him to show you which servant in the Parable of the Tenants you would be and why.

Faithful with Friends and Family

Day 17

"For God said, 'Honor your father and mother."
(Matthew 15:4)

Dream Manual: Read Matthew 15:3–9 and Proverbs 1:8–9 and 13:1.

Reading the words *"honor your father and mother"* may bring out many different emotions for you. Perhaps you have a great relationship with your parents and honoring them is something you already do quite well. Or maybe you don't have a relationship with one or both of you parents, or there is tension with them and the idea of "honoring" them seems impossible to you. No matter where you find yourself between these extremes, God wants us to honor our families. In fact, I've often thought that when I stand before Jesus in eternity He's going to be much more concerned with how I treated my family, the people closest to me, than with how many books I sold or how "successful" I was.

The way we treat our families shows a lot about our true character—who we are when no one is watching. Does that thought scare you like it scares me? It's easy to be impatient with our families, isn't it? Often it's because we know they'll love us no matter what. But when we mistreat them, take them for granted, or disrespect them, what does it say to God about our readiness and ability to be used by Him in greater ways? Being faithful with our families actually prepares us for living out our big dreams, and it is one of God's big dreams for us.

Some of you may have families who aren't Christians or who are just really hard to get along with. Honoring them doesn't mean you have to agree with, model yourself after, or even have a close relationship with all of them. But it does mean treating them with love and respect. When we do so, we show God that we can be faithful with what He's given us and that we are ready for more. It also allows us to be a witness and blessing to our families and a true example of God's love.

This principle applies not only to your parents but to your siblings and extended family as well. God wants to use you to be a light to the world, and what better place to start than with the people He's given you for life—your family? But what does honoring our parents look like practically? How can we honor our families more starting today? Here are two simple steps you can take this week to honor your family and live out one of God's big dreams for your life.

Pray for Them

No matter what you family situation is, we all have access to the incredible power of prayer. Take time today and each day to pray for your family, especially your parents and siblings. Even if your relationship is strained or there are unresolved issues, lift these people up to God, and ask Him to bless them. You may even find your heart towards them softens as you spend this time in prayer. Sometimes the thing that changes most when we pray is ourselves rather than our circumstances. My grandparents have set an amazing example for me in this area. Each day they pray for all of their children, grandchildren, and great-grandchildren by name, and there are over 40 of us on each side of the family! What a blessing.

Express your Love

When is the last time you let your family members know you loved them? For some of you, doing so may be as simple as telling your mom, dad, brother, or sister how much you love them and what they mean to you. For others, it may mean sending a card or letter expressing your love and appreciation or your desire to restore a broken relationship. There are many ways we can reach out and show love to our families: by lending a helping hand, buying a small gift, or taking them out for dinner or a movie. What can you do to express your love this week?

Family, as difficult as it can be, is a gift from God. Learn to be faithful with the ones you were given, knowing one day you may have your own. The trials you learn to overcome now will strengthen you for the future.

Dream Journal

1. Write out a short prayer for your immediate family here:

2. How does it make you feel to think about expressing love to your family? Why?

3. Describe what you hope your future family will look like.

Meet the Dream-Giver

1. Ask Jesus to show you which member of your family, immediate or extended, He'd like you to pray for today.

2. If Jesus were to give one of your family members a gift, what would it be and why? (Consider sharing this gift with that person.)

Day 18

"You have heard that it was said, 'Love your neighbor and hate your enemy.' But I tell you: Love your enemies and pray for those who persecute you." (Matthew 5:43–44)

Dream Manual: Read Matthew 5:38–48.

She absolutely hated me. It was obvious by the way she looked at me with disdain in her eyes and spoke in cold, unfriendly tones. When I asked her how she was doing she replied, "Fine. I'm just getting so tired of this." Her answer sounded vague, but to me it was like a gun loaded with bullets of anger and frustration, pointed directly at me.

"Is there anything I can do to help?" I asked sincerely.

"No, I think you've done enough."

It had been two weeks since she had shut herself off from me completely. I didn't know why it happened, just that it had. When I tried to ask her why she was upset with me, she pretended everything was fine, robbing me of any hope of making things right. And yet I had to see her every Tuesday evening at Bible study and every Sunday morning at church. I had to preach with her in the audience, seemingly choking on every word I spoke. I had to be her friend. So this is what it means to love your enemies?

When Jesus talks about loving our enemies I don't think we really get what He's saying. The reason we don't get it is because we naturally avoid people that don't like us. If they don't like us, why would we hang out with them? We'll just go find someone who does like us, and hang out with them instead. I've learned through several experiences in my life that this method doesn't work. If this was what Jesus wanted us to do He could have said, "Avoid your enemies, and pray for them in the quiet and safety of a group of friends that love and adore you." But that's not what He said. His call is much higher and much harder.

If we want to see our dreams fulfilled, and if we want God to put us in charge of many things—as we read about in the Parable of the Talents—we need to be faithful with our enemies. We need to love those people who don't even like us. I'll say that one more time: *Jesus calls us to love the people that don't even like us.* Here's the tricky part. In order to show love to someone, you actually have to hang out with that person. I know. It's shocking, isn't it? And guess what? Avoiding someone so you don't end up facing conflict is not showing love. In fact, when we try to avoid people we don't like, God often finds a way to put them right in front of us again and again, until we get it right.

The girl I told you about earlier was someone I had to see two or three times a week for six months straight. She was one of two, that's right, two girls my age in the church I was working at, and it was my job to mentor her. I'll be honest, hanging out with her was the last thing I wanted to do, but through it I learned the meaning of this verse for the first time in my life: *"If you love those who love you, what reward will you get? Are not even the tax collectors doing that?"* (Matthew 5:46). Jesus asks us to do the impossible—to love those who hate us. But I can tell you first hand, *He* makes it possible and worth it!

Six months after I left the church and said goodbye to that girl, I received an email from her. In it she apologized for the way she had treated me. But even more amazingly, she said that looking back she could see I really did love her and thanked me for showing God's love to her. Wow, what a miracle. Had I avoided her, she may not have experienced God's love in the way she did. But because of my faithfulness to God's call in this area, her heart was changed. Now don't get me wrong, I'm not saying I did this on my own! Not a chance. It was 100% God and the power of His Holy Spirit that allowed me to show love instead of hatred to her. But after reading that email again and again, I'm glad I was able to put my pride aside and be obedient to Jesus' words in this passage.

Whom in your life might God be using to teach you how to love your enemies? What would happen if, instead of avoiding those people who were difficult to be around, you began praying for them and actively showing God's love to them? How could it change not only their heart but yours as well? Take a moment, and make a list of the people in your life who are difficult to love. Maybe you can think of a friend who hurt you in the past, a family member who broke your trust, a leader that made you feel insignificant, a kid at school or work that just annoys you.

Now spend some time praying for each one of these individuals. Pray for these people by name. Ask God to bless them and use you to bring His love into their lives. It may feel like you have to literally choke the words out, but it's the first step towards truly loving your enemies.

It goes without saying that Jesus set the ultimate example for us in this area. Even when he was beaten, mocked, tortured, and ultimately murdered he spoke these words of love to his killers: *"Father forgive them, for they do not know what they are doing"* (Luke 23:34). Talk about choking on your words. I can barely muster a kind thought when someone cuts me off in traffic! Jesus' example is perfect and only attainable with His help, which is why we need to pray and ask His Holy Spirit to empower us. And when we are faithful in this way, God will continue to entrust us with more kingdom responsibility and opportunities that are beyond our wildest dreams.

Dream Journal

1. Make a list of the people in your life who are the most difficult to love.

2. How can you love at least one of these people in a practical way this week?

3. Why is it difficult to love those who don't like us or rub us the wrong way?

Meet the Dream-Giver

1. Ask Jesus to remind you of a time when you did love someone who was hard to love. How did that feel? What was the result?

2. Ask God to give you a picture of a gift He would like to give to one of the people on your "hard-to-love" list.

FREE TO DREAM PART 1—WHAT HOLDS YOU BACK?

Day 19

"*It was for freedom that Christ has set us free.*"
(Galatians 5:1)

Dream Manual: Read Psalm 51.

Each and every one of us carries a dream, because we carry the image of God. Remember when we talked about creation and how God was the first big dreamer and we're made like Him? It's in our DNA to dream. However, there are always obstacles that threaten to hold us back from living out our dreams. These obstacles come in many different forms, but some of the most powerful ones are hurt, fear, and guilt. Today we're going to focus on identifying the things in our lives that may hold us back from accomplishing our goals so that we can get rid of them once and for all.

When I was in elementary school I was not a popular kid. I was the one that got left out of the soccer game at recess. I was the one whom other kids made fun of and laughed at. They used to call me Heather "dweeb" because my last name was Wiebe and it really hurt my young, tender heart. At the end of each day I'd go home, run into my room, slam the door, and cry. All I wanted was to be loved and accepted—to know I was okay and people liked me. It made me insecure when my classmates didn't like me. I was afraid to be myself, and I carried that fear into junior high as well. I went into a new school trying hard to be liked, but the same thing happened all over again. I was rejected, and it left me feeling hurt and scared.

As I got into my late teens and started thinking about pursuing some of my dreams, many of those fears and insecurities came back. Every time I wanted to step out and take a risk, I felt paralyzed by fear. What if it didn't work out? What if I failed? What if people thought I was a fool? What if I made the wrong decision? And you know what all of the fear and hurt did? It caused me to make some really bad decisions—decisions based on pleasing people instead of pleasing God. And you know what that did? It made me feel a lot of guilt and shame, because I knew I wasn't living the life God had for me. Instead of thinking about what God wanted, I was driven by popularity, reputation, and the praise of people. It was a vicious cycle: hurt from the past and fear of what others thought led to sin, which led to guilt, which led to more hurt and fear.

Can you relate to this cycle? Have you been hurt by people in the past? Maybe friends let you down. Or maybe a family member, a stranger, or a person of the opposite sex made you feel worthless. Are you afraid to step out and be yourself because of these hurts?

Or maybe you've made some big mistakes in your life, and the guilt just won't go away. The Bible says, *"All have sinned and fall short of the glory of God"* (Romans 3:23). None of us is perfect. But if we don't forgive ourselves the way God has, our guilt can keep us from living the abundant life He has in store for us. Not only will our sin make us feel guilty, but it will also rob us of the joy and hope God has for us if we are unwilling to let Him take the guilt away.

Today I want you to ask God about the things that might be holding you back from living your big dream. I want you to think about why you're afraid to be yourself. I want you to be honest with Him about the hurt you may carry from experiences when you feel He left you or let you down. I want you to bring your hurt, guilt and shame to God and allow him to take it away. Lay it all before Him holding nothing back.

King David was really good at expressing his honest emotions to God. Take some time to read a chapter from the book of Psalms and see if you can spot any lines that show the hurt, fear, or guilt David may have feeling when he wrote. Here is one example: *"Hide your face from my sins and blot out all my iniquity. Create in me a pure heart, O God, and renew a steadfast spirit within me. Do not cast me from your presence or take your Holy Spirit from me. Restore to me the joy of your salvation and grant me a willing spirit, to sustain me."* (Psalm 51: 9–12)

What emotions do you see displayed by King David? I see all of the things we've talked about today. I hear the hurt David has as he asks God to *"restore...the joy of your salvation."* I hear the fear in his voice when he begs God, *"Do not cast me from your presence,"* and I hear the guilt when he speaks the words *"Hide your face from my sins."* Yet David's baggage from the past doesn't stop him from finding freedom and moving on to do amazing things in God's kingdom. David was called a "man after God's heart," and I know it wasn't because he was perfect. It was because he brought all of his hurt, fear, and guilt to God and allowed his heavenly Father to heal him.

Hopefully today's lesson will help you identify the things in your life that may be holding you back from living your dreams. Take some extra time today as you journal and ask God to show you what may be holding you back from taking the next step towards your dream. Tomorrow we'll find out how to let go of these things and move forward freely into the amazing plan God has for you!

Dream Journal

1. What is one thing you feel may be holding you back from pursuing your big dreams?

2. Why does that thing have such a hold on you?

3. Find a verse or two you can write down or memorize to encourage you in this area of weakness and challenge.

Meet the Dream-Giver

1. Imagine yourself bringing this weakness to Jesus. What would He do with it when you hand it to him?

2. How do you feel after you've given it to Him?

Free to Dream Part 2—Letting Go

Day 20

"It is for freedom that Christ has set us free. Stand firm then and do not let yourselves be burdened by a yoke of slavery." (Galatians 5:1)

Dream Manual: Read Galatians 5 and John 8:31–36.

Yesterday we spent some time identifying hurt, fear, and guilt that may be holding you back from pursing your dreams. I hope you were able to identify some of those obstacles, not so you can dwell on them and feel even worse, but so you can experience true freedom from them. God wants to set you free, and if you allow Him to, He will! The process may take time or it may happen in an instant, but either way freedom is God's promise to you.

But aren't we set free when we first accept the gift of salvation and commit our lives to Christ? Why do we need more freedom? First of all, we are set free once and for all when we say yes to Jesus. At that moment it's as though Jesus unlocks the door to the prison cell our sin has kept us trapped in. However, many Christians, myself included, don't choose to stand up and walk out of the cell. Instead we sit there, surrounded by all the fear, hurt, and guilt—feeling stuck. In some ways, we become comfortable there, and instead of walking in the freedom

Christ has given, we live like we're still prisoners to our sin. Does this sound familiar to you?

Can you relate to the Psalmist when he said, *"My guilt has overwhelmed me like a burden too heavy to bear…I am bowed down and brought very low; all day long I go about mourning"* (Psalm 38:4,6)? The amazing thing is that you don't have to stay stuck! Jesus bought your freedom, opened the door, and provided a way out of that dark cell. *"It was for freedom that Christ has set us free!"*

All of that sounds pretty wonderful, but the question is how? How do we find the strength to stand up and walk away from our past— from our fears, addictions, guilt, and hurt? In John 8:32, Jesus gives us the answer: *"Then you will know the truth and the truth will set you free"* What keeps us stuck are the lies we believe about ourselves and our true identities. For me, the problem was believing I wasn't good enough and that I would always be left behind. When I finally identified these lies, God spoke a powerful truth to me. He said, "Heather, I was left behind so you would never have to be." Hearing that truth spoken directly and specifically to my situation changed me and gave me the strength to walk out of my prison cell and into the abundant life God had for me. Change isn't always easy, and sometimes I'm tempted go back to my old way of thinking, but as I remind myself of God's truth about me, I find the strength to live in the freedom that He paid such a high price for me to have.

What lies have you been believing about yourself? Here are some common ones Satan uses against us:

- You're not good enough
- You've screwed up too many times for God to forgive
- God obviously doesn't love you if He let you go through that difficult experience or loss
- You'll never be successful
- You'll always be stuck in the sin you secretly struggle with

Take a moment and ask the Holy Spirit to help you identify the lies you've been believing about yourself or about God. Once you do, ask God to speak His truth directly to your situation. Maybe this process means searching His word for a verse relating directly to your struggle and memorizing it or writing it down and looking at it daily. The process may take time, or it may be an instant release, but either way my prayer for you is that you'd be able to echo these words written by David in Psalm 40:1–2: *"I waited patiently for the Lord; he turned to me and heard my cry. He lifted me out of the slimy pit, out of the mud and mire; he set my feet on a rock and gave me a firm place to stand."*

Dream Journal

1. Why do you think Paul makes such an obvious statement in Galatians 5:1? What is the point he's trying to make?

2. What things are keeping you stuck in the prison cell when Jesus has already paid the price and opened the door for you? (What fears, hurts, guilt?)

3. What truth do you need to hear God speak to you today?

Meet the Dream-Giver

1. If you were to meet with Jesus today, where would it be and why?

2. Where is Jesus in the picture? Try to get as close to Him as you can.

3. What would He say to you or do to help set you free?

Day 21

"Those who cleanse themselves…will be instruments for special purposes, made holy, useful to the Master and prepared to do any good work." (2 Timothy 2:21)

Dream Manual: Read the verses included in the lesson as you go through it.

We've spent the last couple of days not only defining what God's dreams for us are but also learning how to be faithful with what He's given us (family, friends, enemies, etc). Today is more practically related to how we can actually get closer to our end goal. There are steps we can take that will bring us much closer to living our big dream. It's all about being ready.

Here's an equation for you to think about. (Don't worry. There's no math involved. I promise.)

Preparation + Opportunity = Success

What is the one factor in this equation we have some level of control over? It's not "success," because that's an end result we can't force or make happen. It's not "opportunity," because we can't control our circumstances or know when or where a new opportunity may come from. So that leaves "preparation." This is the one factor we can practically work towards as we pursue our big dreams and God's call on our lives.

So the questions is, how can we prepare ourselves so that when an opportunity comes knocking, we'll be ready and success will be the end result? Here are three Biblical ways to get prepared: prayer, positive words, and practical steps.

PRAYER: Read Philippians 4:6–7.

If you can get these two verses, I mean really get them at a heart level, you will be set for life! How often are we anxious for God to bring the next step into our lives instead of trusting Him for it? I am so guilty of being anxious. When God first opened the door for me to begin living my dream of a full-time speaking ministry, I couldn't help but worry about when my next opportunity would come along. Instead of worrying, these verses instruct us to cover our dreams and desires in prayer. When you're anxious for the next step, tell Jesus. Lay your worry at His feet. Your hopes and dreams are safe in the hands of your Father, and in return for your anxiety, He gives you His peace. When we bring our requests to Jesus in prayer, it reminds us that we can't and don't need to try and control our futures. All we can do is be prepared so that when He reveals the next step, we're ready to take it.

POSITIVE WORDS: Read Proverbs 15:4.

When you speak to others about your dream and your future, are you speaking words of hope and faith or words of discouragement and doubt? Do you know how powerful these words are? Another way to be prepared is to begin to speak words of life over yourself and your dreams. A habit I've recently developed is speaking these words over myself, especially when I'm feeling down or discouraged: "Heather, you are blessed and highly favored." It's amazing how my emotions will come into line with the truth and authority of God's word as I speak it out loud. Proverbs 15:4 promises that when we speak healing and truth the result is *"a tree of life."* It also promises that words of doubt *"crush the spirit."* How are your words preparing you for the next step in the fulfillment of your God-given dreams? Are they bringing life or crushing your spirit? Are they words of faith, helping you to be confident in what you hope for and sure of what you don't yet see? (Hebrews 11:1) Before I'd even started writing this book, I chose these words for my business card and website as a declaration over myself: "Heather Boersma– Speaker, Author, Dreamer." Each time I see them or speak them, they motivate me to continue on this journey and prepare myself for the opportunities God will bring.

PRACTICAL STEPS: Read Luke 12:35.
This step will look very different for each of us. For the person described in the verses in Luke, being ready meant being dressed, having a lamp burning, and being at the door. What does being ready mean for you? How can you practically be ready for the next opportunity God will bring? Is there a step you can take? A person doing your dream job you can ask to be your mentor? A place you can volunteer where your gifts will be used and grown? For me, this step was the most fun, because I love making a list and getting the tasks done. Why not make a list for yourself of all the practical things you can do this week to get ready for the next opportunity God may bring? You may be surprised to see there's a lot you can do right now to get ready!

Dream Journal

1. Which of the three principles listed is your strength? Which is your weakness? Why?

2. How did Jesus model these three principles in His own life to prepare for what He was called to do?

3. Make a list of the practical steps you can take this week to get ready.

Meet the Dream-Giver

1. Ask Jesus what piece of clothing He wants you to put on to get ready for the next step He has for you. What does this clothing represent?

Day 22

"To obey is better than sacrifice."
(I Samuel 15:20)

Dream Manual: Read 1 Samuel 15.

Do you know what your first words were? I've always loved to talk and started speaking in full sentences at 18 months old. My first two sentences were, "You make me nervous" and "Dad, you build a house for me?" I'm pretty sure hearing those words from me made my parents nervous! I mean, where do kids come up with this stuff? Though my first words were a little out of the ordinary, the first word many children learn to say is "no." When parents hear this word, I imagine they feel somewhat discouraged or disappointed. The word could have been "dada," "mama," or even "yes"! But "no" is actually a very important word. Perhaps the first word many learn as children is the first word we forget how to use effectively when we grow up.

Why do we feel the pressure, even from infancy, to always say "yes"? Why are we taught that saying "no" is bad and saying "yes" is good? Why does the church–the body of Christ–often push us to be "Yes-People"? Is this really what God wants from us?

I realize this is a difficult topic because it addresses the issue of our motivation for doing the things we do, and no one can judge the motives of a man but God himself. But I challenge you to think about why we say yes to the things we say yes to? Is it to impress God? Earn His love? Impress other believers? Earn their respect? One way to better understand the idea of motivation is to look at the difference between "obedience and sacrifice" in the story of King Saul, which you read today.

"But I did obey the Lord,' Saul said. 'I went on the mission the Lord assigned me…the soldiers took sheep and cattle from the plunder, the best of what was devoted to God, in order to sacrifice them to the Lord your God.' But Samuel replied: 'Does the Lord delight in burnt offerings and sacrifices as much as in obeying the voice of the Lord? To obey is better than sacrifice, and to heed is better than the fat of rams.'" (I Samuel 15:20–22)

Here's a thought: The right action, at the wrong time and for the wrong reason, is the wrong action. This is the difference between obedience and sacrifice. In the story you read today Saul told Samuel the reason he let his men keep some of the plunder from battle was to give it to God as a burnt offering. That in and of itself was not a bad thing to do. However, in making this decision, Saul disobeyed God's first command, which was to destroy everyone and everything and keep nothing. How does this somewhat obscure story relate to your life?

Saul said "yes" to keeping sheep and livestock as an offering to God when he should have said "no." Even though giving a burnt offering was a "good thing," *the reason* Saul did it was wrong. His motivation was selfish, and his heart was rebellious to the Lord. Right before this conversation with Samuel, Saul had just finished building a monument to honor *himself* instead of God! And right after Samuel scolds him, Saul says, *"I have sinned. I violated the Lord's command and your instructions. I was afraid of the people and so I gave in to them"* (1 Sam 15:24). Here Saul admits the reason he said yes to keeping some of the plunder was because of his desire to please and impress "the people" rather than God.

How often do we do the right thing for the wrong reason? Do you ever say yes to impress others and honor yourself instead of God?

There is a difference between obedience (saying yes to God's voice and commands) and sacrifice (saying yes to what you/others deem to be "right" or "good" things). Sometimes it is better to say no.

Learning to say no is a skill God values. There was a time in my life when I didn't know how to say no. Every time I was asked to be involved at church, help out on a team, or volunteer in another ministry, I said yes. I felt I was a "good person" and a "strong Christian" because of these choices. Until I realized that by saying yes to doing all this good stuff, I was actually saying no to being with God and doing what He was specifically calling me to do. Is your yes to good deeds inadvertently a no to intimacy with or obedience to God?

As you chase your big dreams there will be many opportunities to be involved in great things. It is important for you to remember the difference between obedience and sacrifice when these opportunities come up and to ask for God's direction about each one. Understand that sometimes He may guide you to say no, even though it looks like a great opportunity. Though saying yes might make us look good to others and feel important, God is not impressed by our actions. He is most pleased with a heart that is first and foremost obedient to His voice. *"This is love for God: to obey his commands"* (1 John 5:3).

Dream Journal

1. Make a list of all the things you are involved with right now, including school, church, and extracurricular activities.

2. Looking at this list, are there any areas where you feel you could/should have said no instead of yes? Why?

3. Is spending quality time with God one of your top priorities in terms of time? Explain.

Meet the Dream-Giver

1. Ask God to show you one area of your life where you need to learn to say "no."

2. Ask Him how He feels about the amount of time and energy you are putting into your relationship with Him right now.

WEAKNESSES—YOUR GREATEST STRENGTHS?

Day 23

"I can do everything through him who gives me strength."
(Philippians 4:13)

Dream Manual: Read 1 Corinthians 1:25–31 and Romans 8:28–39.
My struggle with lust started as a direct result of my rebellion toward
God. The summer after I graduated from high school I met a guy
whom I really liked but knew wasn't right for me. I'd never been in a
relationship before, because I really wanted to only date the man I was
going to marry. I didn't see dating as something to be taken lightly. But
that summer I got tired of waiting for "Mr. Right," so I disobeyed God's
voice. I even wrote this in my journal when the relationship began: "I
really don't think this guy is marriage material, but I just want to have
some fun." What followed that one decision was three years of trial,
hardship, and a huge step back in my relationship with God.

The real trouble started when I became involved in an unhealthy
physical relationship with this guy. Though we never actually slept
together, we constantly pushed and broke our physical boundaries and I
became caught up in a personal battle with lust. At the end of three years
I finally realized how stuck I'd become and cried out for God to save

me. Through the help of close friends and lots of prayer, accountability, and the power of the Holy Spirit I was set free from the relationship and eventually my personal struggle as well.

However, even after I overcame my battle with lust, I still carried a lot of shame for the choices I'd made, both in the relationship and on my own. Shame felt like a big black cloud looming over my life—a three-year mistake I could never erase. But I was wrong. What the devil meant for evil and destruction, God was going to redeem and use for good! God began challenging me to confess my personal struggle to several of my friends, and though I was terrified and feared they would judge me, I found the opposite to be true. Not only were they loving and accepting in their responses, but they admitted they were struggling with some of the very same issues! Through exposing my greatest weakness, God gave them the courage and strength to overcome their personal struggles as well. My greatest weakness had become a great strength!

This principle is exactly what Paul was referring to in 2 Corinthians 12:9–10 when he wrote, *"But he said to me, 'My grace is sufficient for you, for my power is made perfect in weakness.' Therefore I will boast all the more gladly about my weaknesses, so that Christ's power may rest on me. That is why, for Christ's sake, I delight in weaknesses, in insults, in hardships, in persecutions, in difficulties. For when I am weak, then I am strong."* We are most effective for God not when we attain personal perfection, but when we allow God's grace to heal our brokenness and use those experiences to help others. Then God truly receives all the honor and glory, and His kingdom, not ours, is built.

What are your greatest weaknesses? Maybe you have a secret sin like the one I struggled with, or maybe your issue relates to a personality trait or tendency you have. Maybe you feel too shy, too loud, too scared, too proud, too selfish, or too accommodating. Perhaps it's not a sin you've committed but something that's been done *to* you (e.g., physical or emotional abuse, betrayal, rejection, etc.). Whatever your issue is, know that it's not too much for God's grace to redeem. It's not so detestable He can't wash it clean and give you a new start. If you allow Jesus to heal you, the very things Satan meant for harm, God will use for good!

My best friend, Alisha, said some powerful words to me when I was finally free from my unhealthy relationship and struggle with lust. She said, "Heather, through Christ, your greatest weakness will become your greatest ministry." She was right. Over the past six years God has given me countless opportunities to share my story with thousands of teenagers and see many of them set free from their personal struggles. If I would've kept my sin a secret and never confessed it to God and my close friends, my relationship with God as well as His purposes for my life could still be on hold.

How happy would Satan be if he could keep you stuck in your sin and shame? He wants to keep you from all your dreams and all God has in store for you. John 10:10 says, *"The thief comes only to steal and kill and destroy; I have come that they may have life."* Don't allow Satan to steal another moment by keeping you stuck in fear and shame. God's grace is more than enough for the deepest, darkest secrets you may have. Today is the day to bring them into the light. Now is the time to see your greatest weakness transformed into your greatest strength!

Dream Journal

1. What is one weakness you have that you feel God could never use or redeem?

2. How do you feel when you think about exposing that part of yourself to God? To others?

3. What is one step you can take towards seeing this weakness transformed into a strength and perhaps become part of your future ministry?

Meet the Dream-Giver

1. Ask God how He sees you today, with all of your strengths and weaknesses. What stands out to Him the most?

PART THREE

UNLOCKING
YOUR
Dream

THE KEY IS INTIMACY

Day 24

"Love the Lord your God with all your heart and with all your soul and with all your strength." (Deuteronomy 6:5)

Dream Manual: Read Luke 10: 38–42.

Getting locked out of the house is the most frustrating thing in the world and something I happen to be really good at. When I was in junior high, I used to take the bus home from school and many times I would walk up to the front door and realize I didn't have my keys. I would then proceed to check every other door and window to see if there was some other way into the house. Each time I would kick myself for not having my keys and wish that I was inside, eating a snack and watching some after-school TV. Instead I was stuck, sometimes in the cold, waiting for my parents to get home from work, roll their eyes at me, unlock the door and let me in. In those moments it felt as though everything good was on one side of the door, and I was stuck on the other. And try as I might to break in another way, it was impossible without the right key.

What if I told you I know the key that can unlock the door to not only the fulfillment of all your wildest dreams but the best life possible? Would you be interested? What would you be willing to give up for a key like this? Comfort? Money? Time? Hobbies? This key is intimacy with God.

According to the Merriam-Webster dictionary, the definition of *intimacy* is "marked by very close association, contact, or familiarity; marked by a warm friendship developing through long association; of a very personal or private nature."

Is this the kind of relationship you have with God? Are you in close contact with your heavenly Father? Do you have a warm friendship with Jesus? A personal and relationship with the Holy Spirit? I fall short of this kind of relationship with God sometimes. But intimacy like this is truly the key to seeing our dreams come true.

As we get to know God more intimately, we understand His character and learn to trust Him more deeply. And as we trust Him more, we are transformed into the people He created us to be. When this happens, we are available and able to walk out the purpose and plan He set out for us when He first created us.

Here are three more reasons that intimacy with God is key:

Intimacy allows us to hear God's voice.
We've already talked about listening prayer in the last thirty days, and hopefully it's something you've been practicing. I pray you are hearing God speak to you, because who better to direct you to the next steps you need to take than the one who sees the whole picture? God doesn't just see where our lives are at today, this week, or even this month. He sees the beginning, middle, and end! Sometime we may feel like we're stuck in some kind of maze, but God is the one who sits up top looking down on us as we try to get through. And what better way to find our next turn than to ask the one who can see the way we need to go? Spending time with God daily allows us to get to know His voice better so that when He asks us to do something, we can obey Him more readily. The more we walk in obedience to God, the closer we get to living out the big dreams He has for us.

Intimacy reminds us of who we are.
Sometimes in the quest for our dreams we get lost. Maybe we experience

failure, heartbreak, or discouragement. Maybe someone tears us down with harsh words or we start to feel like we're not good enough. Intimacy with God reminds of our true identity in Christ. As we read His word, hear His voice, and share our hearts with Him, we are reminded of His great love for us. We are reminded of who we are and how valuable we are. And who are we?

- We bear the image of God (Genesis 1:27)
- We are fearfully and wonderfully made (Psalm 139:14)
- We are children of God (John 1:12)
- We are Gods' friends (John 15:15)
- We are heirs of God and co-heirs with Christ (Romans 8:17)

All of these truths and so many more are found in the Bible, and when we spend time with God, we are reminded of our value and purpose. Without an understanding of who we are, how can we know where we are going? Intimacy with God keeps us from losing track of both of those things.

Intimacy gives us perspective.

We get caught up in the here and now. We forget that this earth is not our home and our final destination is heaven and eternity with God. As we spend time talking and listening to God, reading His word, and sitting in His presence, He helps us to fix our eyes on eternity. In 2 Corinthians 4:18, we read, *"So we fix our eyes not on what is seen, but on what is unseen. For what is seen is temporary, but what is unseen is eternal."* The only way we can change our perspective is by spending daily time with God. The world is loud and bright and full of distractions. If we want to remain focused on our final goal–heaven–we need God's help.

Dream Journal

1. Find three more verses that describe who we are in Christ and write down the references.

2. What has your experience with hearing God's voice been like lately? How could it be improved?

3. In what areas of your life do you need some God-perspective right now and why?

Meet the Dream-Giver

1. Ask Jesus to give you His eyes to see the circumstances you are facing today. How does He see them differently than you do?

2. Ask Jesus what one thing is that you can do today to grow a more intimate relationship with Him.

WORSHIP THE DREAM-GIVER, NOT THE DREAM

Day 25

"Don't be deceived dear brothers and sisters. Every good and perfect gift is from above, coming down from the Father of the heavenly lights, who does not change like shifting shadows." (James 1:16–17)

Dream Manual: Read Exodus 20:1–6

What is the best gift you ever received? Maybe it was a birthday or Christmas present, or perhaps it was a gift that was totally unexpected or undeserved. One of the most memorable gifts I ever received was a white gold necklace with a diamond pendant from my husband (who was my boyfriend at the time). When I opened the gift, I was completely surprised and thought it was the most beautiful thing ever. However, what made me love it most was *who it was from*, not what it was. Sure, it was a beautiful piece of jewelry but more importantly, it reflected the love and generosity of the giver. If I loved the necklace more than the person who gave it to me, I'd be missing the whole point.

So often we worship the gifts God gives us rather than Him—the giver. Our verse today, James 1:16–17, says *"Don't be deceived dear brothers and sisters. Every good and perfect gift is from above, coming down from the Father of the heavenly lights, who does not change like shifting shadows."* It's interesting that this verse begins with the words, *"Don't be deceived."* These words warn us not to be tricked into worshiping the things, people, or dreams God gives us instead of worshiping Him—the one who gives them to us! When we value the gift more than the giver it's called "idolatry." This is a big word that basically refers to worshipping anything more than God. An idol could be our friends, family, stuff, or even ourselves! Our big dream can become one of those idols too.

How do we keep this from happening to our big dreams? By holding them with open hands. When God gives us a desire, a dream, a vision for our lives, we need to hold it loosely. If we start to close our fingers around it and clench it tightly, we squeeze the life right out of it. It becomes an idol, something that takes away from our relationship with God rather than causing us to thank Him and love Him even more. The gift reflects the heart of the giver, doesn't it? God doesn't give us good things so that we'll grab onto them, claim them as our own, and forget all about Him. He gives them to us because He loves us and wants to draw us into a closer, more intimate relationship with Him. If we miss the point and don't keep an open hand, He may have to pry our finger off and remove the gift—a process that can be quite painful.

I experienced this process first hand a few years ago. It was right around the time I first started speaking to youth and young adults. God gave me a dream to be a full-time speaker and writer and placed an amazing opportunity in my life to go on a tour across Canada, speaking to thousands of youth. I went and had an amazing time, but in the process I started to love speaking and want it so much that I sort of lost sight of God. I stopped asking Him about his plans and His next steps for my ministry and instead made my own plans. I closed my hand around the gift He'd given me and started worshipping my dream of being a speaker rather than the one who'd given me the dream. As a result, God began to close the doors for a speaking ministry, and I saw my dream begin to die. He didn't do it to be mean or cruel—quite the opposite actually. He did it to draw me back to Him and to His heart. God is a jealous God, and when we give our time, attention, love, and energy to anything more than Him, He will do what it takes to refocus us. In the end, I had to let go of my dream for a season so I could focus on worshipping God rather than the dream. A few years later, God started to open new doors and revive my dream, but I first had to learn to hold it with an open hand while loving Him and thanking Him for the dream daily.

In the end, nothing else matters besides knowing God. How well do you know Him? Do you realize His heart longs for you? Do you know He is jealous for your time and attention? Do you know He wants to speak to you? And most importantly, if you met him today, would you recognize Him? The greatest fulfillment we will ever experience, now or in eternity, comes not from seeing our dreams come true, but from loving and being loved by God. There is no greater satisfaction than what we will feel when we see the unveiled face of our Savior in eternity. I think these lines from the band *Hillsong United* say it well: *"Though I have not seen him, my heart knows him well."* Does your heart know Him well, or have you made idols of the gifts He's given you?

Dream Journal

1. Are you worshipping your dream or the Dream-Giver more in your life right now?

2. What is one thing in your life that has or could become an idol— something you give more time and attention to than God?

3. How can you make sure that thing doesn't become an idol?

4. If God was to take away your big dream for a time, how would you feel/react?

Meet the Dream-Giver

1. Ask God to show you anything in your life that is coming before Him.

2. Confess these idols to Him, and picture yourself laying them at His feet. How does Jesus respond?

LIVE IN THE MOMENT WHILE WAITING FOR YOUR MOMENT

Day 26

"Why, you do not even know what will happen tomorrow. What is your life? You are a mist that appears for a little while and then vanishes." (James 4:14)

Dream Manual: Read Matthew 6:25–34 and James 4:13–17.

Abraham was seventy-five years old when God first called him. That day God planted His big dream in Abraham's heart by saying to him, *"I will make you into a great nation and I will bless you; I will make your name great and you will be a blessing."* Pretty amazing promise isn't it? I can only imagine how I'd feel if God spoke those words to me. I'd probably be thinking, "Okay, God. Let's do it! What do I do next? What's the plan?" Well, for Abraham the plan was this: do nothing. Wait for twenty-five—that's right, twenty-five years—and then I'll give you a child. That's a long time to wait. Imagine how Abraham felt as he waited for twenty-five years only to see the beginning of his dream coming true, the birth of his son Isaac. And even 100 years later, when he died at the age of 175, Abraham still didn't get to see the fullness of God's promise to him.

Joseph was seventeen years old when God first gave him his dream. You may remember from earlier in our study that Joseph had to wait until he was thirty years old to see his dream come true. That's thirteen years. And it wasn't an easy thirteen years either. Things got a lot worse before they got better. David's story is similar to Joseph's. When he was a teenager, maybe only fifteen years old, David was chosen to be the future king of Israel. But not until he was thirty years old did he see this dream come true. In the years in between he was hunted by Saul, the current king, and forced into hiding. Talk about needing patience and trust. It must've been hard for both Joseph and David to believe they'd ever see their dreams come true. But they aren't the only ones who had to wait. Even Jesus himself waited thirty years before He began His public ministry, and it only lasted three years!

I hope hearing about these people encourages you to be patient as you wait for your moment and the fulfillment of your big dreams. Maybe you won't have to wait twenty-five years like Abraham or even ten to fifteen, like Joseph and David, but even if you do, I hope you won't let the waiting stop you from living in the moment. Today is a gift you can never get back, and how you live today shows God whether or not you're ready for what He has for your tomorrow. If Joseph hadn't been a slave and a prisoner for many years, perhaps he wouldn't have been the humble leader he was. His faithfulness to God through the time of waiting developed his character and the qualities he would need to be second-in-command of all of Egypt. Joseph was faithful through the whole process, honoring God every step of the way. When the time came—his appointed time—he was ready.

Chris Vallaton, a pastor at Bethel Church in Redding California, said this in one of his sermons: "God takes a long time to act suddenly." What this comment tells me is that I need to be living each moment to the fullest so that when God does act, I'm ready. If I'm too busy feeling sorry for myself, being impatient, or even rebelling against God because He's not doing things my way, I may miss my moment.

What about you? Are you going to be ready when He calls you? Are you embracing all He has for you today, right now, in this season of life? Or are you anxiously waiting for tomorrow? Maybe you're waiting to meet the right person, to find the right job, to start the next phase of your education, or to be a part of the right community. But what about today? What about the here and now and what God has put right in front of you?

In Matthew 6:34, Jesus encourages us not *"to worry about tomorrow, for tomorrow will worry about itself."* Paul further encourages us in James 4:14, saying, *"Now listen, you who say 'Today or tomorrow we will go to this city or that city, spend a year there, carry on business and make money.' Why you do not even know what will happen tomorrow."* All we have is today, and today is a chance for you to grow closer to Jesus. Today is an opportunity for you to love the people God has put in your path. Today will never happen again. Today is a gift.

Dream Journal

1. Rate yourself on the scale below. How well have you been living in the moment (with 0 = always thinking about tomorrow and 10 = fully embracing the present moment)

    0_____10

2. What is one way you can embrace the moment more?

3. How do you respond when God doesn't move at the pace you'd like Him to?

4. How do you think your reaction affects your relationship with Him?

Meet the Dream-Giver

1. Imagine you and Jesus are going for a jog together. Are you moving at the same pace as Him?

2. If you're going faster or slower, what can you change in your life to get on track with Him and His pace?

Day 27

"Consider it pure joy, my brothers and sisters, whenever you face trials of many kinds, because you know that the testing of your faith develops perseverance. Perseverance must finish its work so that you may be mature and complete, not lacking anything." (James 1:2–3)

Dream Manual: Read Matthew 5:1–11.

It was the worst week of my life. My computer crashed, taking with it all my photos and half of a book I was working on. I discovered I had to sell my puppy, the first one I'd ever owned. One of my closest friends decided she no longer loved or trusted me. My husband admitted he'd been keeping some things from me for the first nine months of our marriage. And to top it all off, we were kicked out of our home—the church we'd been volunteering in for the past six months. The irony of the situation was that this year was supposed to be the year for my big dreams to come true. Instead, my dream had officially turned into a nightmare.

Sometimes, in the process of pursuing the dreams God plants in our hearts, we face major challenges. (By sometimes, I mean most times). These challenges happen for a few reasons. Here are some of them:

- Satan hates it when we live the life God has called us to. It's a major threat to him, and he'll do anything to stop it.
- We live in a fallen world where bad things happen without reason.
- We each have a sinful nature, and when we give into it the consequences can be quite painful.

Even when we face these trials the Bible tells us to *"consider it pure joy."* I can tell you for a fact that pure joy was not something I was feeling the week my life fell apart. Pure sadness? Yes. Pure loneliness? Definitely. But pure joy? Nope, not on the list. However the verse doesn't tell us to *feel* pure joy. It says we should *consider* it pure joy. Having joy when life stinks is a choice, not a feeling. Why on earth should we consider trials pure joy, though? Well, because they grow character in us, of course. Not a good enough reason for you?

What if God knows that there are parts of your personality and character that aren't ready for the things He has planned for your future? What if He knows that if you were to get your dream job tomorrow you would fail miserably at it because of some bad habits or weaknesses you possess? Would you want Him to help you get rid of those things before you really mess up? I know I would. The verses in James tell us this is exactly what's happening when we go through difficult situations in life. They develop perseverance in us and perseverance matures and completes us! Trials are like boot camp for our spirits.

Think of it this way. No one runs a marathon without training first. Doing so would be a total disaster. It takes months of training to successfully prepare for a marathon. The same is true in our spiritual lives. The trials we go through train us and prepare us to live out the big dreams God has in store for us. Without going through those difficult times we might not be ready for what's to come, or we may fail miserably because we aren't spiritually mature enough. The pain we go through now is preparing us for future success. And anything the devil meant for evil, God can use for your good if you let Him.

Some of the things I went through that week still don't make sense to me. In fact I'm not sure I will ever fully know why I had to experience what I did. But I do know that God used those events to develop perseverance in me, to mature me, and to prepare me for the next season in my life. I believe they brought me closer to fulfilling my big dreams and one day, maybe only in heaven, I will look back and see the bigger picture. But for now I trust that He uses the difficult times to grow something in me I really need.

But beware! If we choose not to consider our trials pure joy, they can have the reverse effect on us. They can cause us to question our faith and become angry with God. Don't fall into this trap. It's exactly where Satan wants you, and as soon as he gets you there, he'll do everything in his power to keep you there. Being frustrated with God is normal. Questioning Him is not a sin. But we can't expect that our lives will be easy just because we believe in Him. The Bible never promised life would be easy. In fact, eleven out of the twelve disciples were persecuted and killed for their faith in Jesus, and they were His best friends on earth! If they weren't exempt from trials, why should we expect to be? Viewing our challenges with pure joy is a hard choice, but it's one you can make with God's help. And when you do, not only will you rob Satan of all the fun he wants to have messing with your faith, you'll also grow into a stronger and a more mature and complete person—one who is ready to take on the next steps God has for you on the path to your big dreams!

Dream Journal

1. What was the hardest day/week/season of your life?

2. During that time how did you respond, and what did the situation teach you?

3. Are you pursuing your big dreams now, or have you given up because of challenges and trials you may be facing?

Meet the Dream-Giver

1. If there is a specific challenge you are facing right now, ask Jesus to show you what He wants to do for you in that trial.

2. Take some time to ask Jesus to renew your mind and give you a new perspective about the challenges you are currently facing. Perhaps He'll bring a verse to mind or give you a picture or a song to help you find joy in a dark time.

Day 28

"Remember this: Whoever sows sparingly will also reap sparingly, and whoever sows generously will also reap generously." (2 Corinthians 9:6)

Dream Manual: Read Galatians 6:1–10 and 2 Corinthians 9:6–15. The Biblical principle of sowing and reaping is straight-forward in theory. When you give or "sow" generously you will receive or "reap" generously. Sounds pretty easy doesn't it? But how does this principle apply to our dreams? How does it apply to using our dreams to inspire others?

When I first realized my dream was to speak and write full time, I felt very alone. It's not the most common dream, and it's also not something you can just take a university course to learn. I often wished I knew someone who was already living my dream so that I could get advice and model myself after someone. Eventually, after over five years of pursuing my dream, I did find someone who was already successfully doing what I wanted and felt called to do. Connecting with her was what inspired me to actively pursue my dream full-time and gave me confidence that it really was possible to attain my goals. If she could do it, why couldn't I?

After experiencing the benefit of that relationship, I realized I wanted to provide support and encouragement for others too. I began to pray and ask God to put young people in my path who wanted to speak and write full-time, and that's exactly what He did. At first I found it tough to share all the knowledge, ideas, and contacts I'd built up over the past few years, but then I read these words in 2 Corinthians 9:12–13: *"This service that you perform is not only supplying the needs of the Lord's people but is also overflowing in many expressions of thanks to God. Because of the service by which you have proved yourselves, others will praise God for the obedience that accompanies your confession of the gospel of Christ, and for your generosity in sharing with them and with everyone else."* By sharing generously with other dreamers around me, God was given all the glory, and I was sowing into the growth of *His* kingdom, not my own. When we are generous with our dreams and use them to inspire others, our actions show Him our gratitude and cause others to praise God.

What dream has God given you, and how can you help and bless others who have the same dream? In whom could you be investing? Maybe you could simply encourage someone younger than you to believe God has a unique dream for his or her life. Or maybe you could find someone who is pursing the same goal as you and, instead of viewing that person as competition, work together to lift each other up. Our culture tells us that in order to get higher we need to push others down, but God's work says the opposite. The more we give, the more we'll receive from Him! The more we honor others and place their needs before our own, the more we'll see our dreams move forward. When we share our time, our wisdom, and our opportunities with others, these choices—instead of putting us behind—will actually move us ahead.

This is exactly what Jesus did with His disciples. He spend much of His three years of active ministry pouring into the lives of twelve young men. Jesus saw the bigger picture and knew that soon He'd be gone and someone else would need to carry His vision forward. He also promised the disciples they would do and see even greater things that He had. (Check out John 14:12.) Jesus wanted to equip the disciples so they could continue the work He began. Who can you pour into this way?

How can you multiply your efforts by joining with others who share your dreams and passions?

A couple of summers ago I was given the opportunity to share my dream, and I'm glad I did so. I was asked to be the speaker for a week at a local Bible camp. I began preparing for my five chapel sessions. As I was praying for the week, I kept thinking about an acquaintance of mine from church who had expressed interest in becoming a full-time speaker and writer. The more I prayed, the more I knew God wanted me to offer her the chance to speak during one of the chapel sessions. I knew it was the Holy Spirit speaking to me, but part of me didn't want to obey. I didn't want the campers and staff to like her better than me or to ask her to speak the following summer instead of me. But all of those thoughts were selfish, and I knew they weren't from God. So I obeyed the Spirit's leading and offered her the chance to speak. She gratefully accepted and did an amazing job sharing with the campers that evening. I don't exactly know the effect this decision had on her or my ministry, but I do believe it was a chance for me to sow generously into God's kingdom, which is a chance I don't want to miss!

Dream Journal

1. Make a list of all the people you know who have similar dreams and goals to you.

2. How can you pour into two or three of these people's lives in the coming week?

3. How did Jesus set an example for you in this area? (Try to find a scripture to prove it!)

Meet the Dream-Giver

1. Ask Jesus how He wants to inspire and encourage you in your dream today.

Day 29

"Therefore, since we are surrounded by such a great cloud of witnesses, let us throw off everything that hinders and the sin that so easily entangles. And let us run with perseverance the race marked out for us, fixing our eyes on Jesus, the pioneer and perfecter of faith." (Hebrews 12:1–2)

Dream Manual: Read Hebrews 11.

I'm not sure what made me do it, but a couple of years ago I decided to run a half-marathon. I've always enjoyed jogging, but little did I know that running thirteen miles is actually more difficult than my leisurely half-hour jogs. I trained for about four months and did most of my training alone. I was living out at a camp at the time and would run for hours by myself on the highway. It was peaceful but often very difficult to stay motivated, as I didn't have a running buddy or even an iPod with good music to keep me company. I started to wonder if I'd really be able to run a half-marathon.

On the day of the race, everything changed. I arrived at the starting line early in the morning to find myself surrounded by thousands of other runners. The energy in the air was electrifying, and my heart pounded with excitement. Suddenly all my doubts and fears about being able to finish the run disappeared. By the time the starting shot was fired, I was ready to go. Not only that, but I ran the race in 2 hours and 13 seconds, only 13 seconds over my goal! There was one point in the two-hour race when I thought about quitting, but as I looked around at the hundreds of other runners and the people cheering us on from the sidewalks and water stations, I knew I could do it.

This is exactly the kind of encouragement Paul is talking about in Hebrews 12:1. As we pursue the big dreams God has planted in our hearts, we need to remember we aren't running this race alone. Millions of dreamers have gone before us, and millions more will follow. The company we keep as dreamers with God is a long and impressive list, as you read in Hebrews 11. We run with some of the greats, like Abraham and Isaac, Jacob and Joseph, Moses and Rahab. Though there may be times in your journey when you feel like me in the middle of that marathon—ready to quit and to take an easier path—don't give up! Just look behind you at the amazing men and women of God who've gone before, and know you are surrounded. Not only that, but find some people to surround yourself with who are also pursuing their God-given dreams, and make them your "running buddies." It's much easier to keep going when we know we're not running alone. It also helps to know what we are running towards. Hebrews 11:13–16 says this:

"All these people were still living by faith when they died. They did not receive the things promised; they only saw them and welcomed them from a distance, admitting that they were foreigners and strangers on earth. People who say such things show that they are looking for a country of their own. If they had been thinking of the country they had left, they would have had opportunity to return. Instead, they were longing for a better country—a heavenly one. Therefore God is not ashamed to be called their God, for he has prepared a city for them."

The race we are running here on earth will not end with worldly success. That is not our goal, nor was it the goal of the great cloud of witnesses who went before us. Our goal is heaven, the "better country" described in Hebrews 11. Perhaps you're discouraged to see that many of the people described in Hebrews 11 didn't get to see their big dreams fulfilled here on earth. Perhaps it makes you want to give up before you've even really started. But the promise God gives to us who run this race is amazing—a heavenly dwelling where we can meet and dwell with God face to face for all of eternity. Though we may experience some of this joy on earth, the completion of it will only come when we reach the heavenly home God has prepared for us. This is why we need to be surrounded by those who are like-minded, whose goal is heaven and all God has for us there. May it be said not just of them but of us as well: *"These were all commended for their faith, yet none of them received what had been promised, since God had planned something better for us so that only together with us would they be made perfect"* (Hebrews 11:39–40).

Dream Journal

1. Which Biblical person inspires you the most and why?

2. Take some time and reread that person's story. What stands out to you/encourages you the most about it?

3. How does it make you feel to know you may not see the fulfillment of all your dreams here on earth?

Meet the Dream-Giver

1. Ask Jesus which Biblical person He see reflected in your life and why.

Day 30

"Now to him who is able to do immeasurably more than all we ask or imagine, according to his power that is at work within us, to him be glory in the church and in Christ Jesus throughout all generations, forever and ever! Amen." (Ephesians 3:20–21)

Dream Manual: Read 2 Corinthians 4.

There is no reason you can't start living God's big dream for your life today. You don't need to wait for everything to fall perfectly into place and see all of the doors opened before you. All you need is to take one step forward—a step you've been led by the Spirit to take. This 30-day journey began with the verses above, from Ephesians 3, and it will end with these verses as well. I hope that by this point you are convinced that God can do *"immeasurably more than all we ask or imagine,"* but today I want to emphasize another part of this passage. This whole journey of living the dream is all for one reason and one reason only— to bring glory to God. Verse 21 says *"to him be the glory in the church and in Christ Jesus throughout all generations, forever and ever."* Not only is this our purpose for our brief time here on earth, but for eternity as well.

116

I heard an amazing story from my friend Amy the other day that illustrates perfectly how living our big dream each day can bring glory to God. I hope it inspires and encourages you as much as it did me.

Amy is 29 years old. She is funny, driven, motivated, and hardworking. Amy works as the office manager for a local construction company; she values her family and friends and loves children. She doesn't have any of her own children yet, but she hopes one day she will. A couple of months ago, through much prayer and seeking the Lord, Amy decided to take five weeks away from work to visit her cousins who work as missionaries in Chad, Africa. What she didn't know is just how much this short trip and small step towards her big dreams would bring glory to God.

Amy spent a lot of her time in Chad helping her cousin homeschool their five children and encouraging her cousin who, like Amy, lives with Type 1 Diabetes. Though she didn't have a specific agenda for her time there, Amy took what God put in front of her each day and was faithful with it.

One afternoon, Amy and her cousin's family went to visit a nearby orphanage run by a local pastor and his wife. They entered the compound and immediately sensed the poverty and need. As they walked around the courtyard, Amy noticed a baby girl, who looked no older than a year, sitting by herself in a dirt breezeway. The sight shocked her, and she wondered why this little one was all alone. After speaking with the pastor, she found out the girl had been abandoned a couple of months earlier. She was very sick, and the workers didn't think she was going to live. Amy's cousin asked to hold her, and the pastor said she could try. Her heart broke as she gently lifted the girl and felt little more than skin and bones in her arms.

After leaving the orphanage, Amy and her cousin wondered what they could do to help this little girl. They decided to buy some formula for her and bring it to the orphanage, but they knew this was only a short-term solution. When Amy left Chad at the end of her trip, her heart ached because she knew this girl would likely not make it to her next birthday. She wondered what the point was. Why had God brought her all the way to Chad, shown her this suffering, and not given her a way to help save this girl's life? Was this really the big dream she'd been hoping and praying for?

A few weeks after her return, Amy received an email from her cousin. In it her cousin informed Amy that she and her family had decided to adopt this little girl. *"Amy, THANK YOU for wanting to go to the orphanage. That day has changed our lives forever! Little did we know, even when you left, how God would work and confirm that she is ours."* Because of Amy's faithfulness to follow where God led that day, she was used to build His kingdom and bring glory to His name.

This is what it means to live God's big dream! When we listen to the Father's voice and obey it—follow where He leads—we will be used to make His kingdom here on earth more like it is in heaven. It's not about making our name known or working for our glory, but to make Jesus' name known and give all the glory to Him, both now and forever. Had Amy not travelled to Chad and not listened to the nudging in her heart to visit the orphanage, that little girl may have died without ever knowing true love.

Dream Journal

1. Reread 2 Corinthians 4:15. What does this verse say about our role in living out God's big dream for our lives?

2. How are you pursuing your big dream today?

3. Write out a prayer, recommitting your big dreams to God and to His glory.

Meet the Dream-Giver

1. Imagine Jesus is giving you a backpack for the next leg of your journey with Him. What three things would be in that backpack?

2. Ask Him what each of those three things represent and why you need them.